LifeSpan

IN THE SPIRIT

A Pre- & Post-Confirmation Programme
for Catholic & Anglican Teenage Christians

by
Dr Stephen Gomez & Revd Jean Kings

with
Revd Mark Earey
Revd Paul Denyer
Annalise DeSouza
John Murphy

Drawings by
Jean Kings & Nick Park

CANDIDATE'S GUIDE

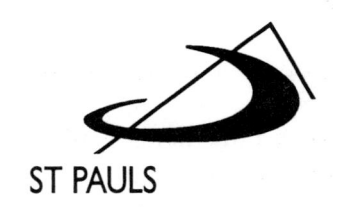

ST PAULS

Many thanks to Revd Dennis Sutton and Sr Teresa Phelan of The Dunstan RE Centre, Bristol for their encouragement and advice; also Revd Canons Alastair Redfern and Robin Protheroe for their constructive criticism.

Cover design by Julian Alexander Quaye

ST PAULS
Middlegreen, Slough SL3 6BT, United Kingdom
Moyglare Road, Maynooth, Co. Kildare, Ireland

© Stephen Gomez & Jean Kings 1995
ISBN 085439 492 3
Printed by Martins The Printers Ltd, Berwick upon Tweed

ST PAULS is an activity of the priests and brothers of the
Society of St Paul who proclaim the Gospel through the media of social communication

Contents

Reaching Confirmation in the Spirit

		Page
1.	Introductions	2
	Celebration of Commissioning	4
2.	Is Anybody There?	6
3.	The Ups and Downs of Life	8
4.	Breakfast TV	10
5.	Bible-bashing	12
6.	What's in a Name?	14
7.	Your Ideal Person	16
8.	Jesus' Life	18
9.	What makes a Christian?	20
10.	Why Did Jesus Have to Die?	24
11.	Taste & See	26
12.	Sponsor Checklist	28
13.	Confirmation Retreat	29

Coming of Age in the Spirit

		Page
14.	Overview	30
15.	Doubt	32
16.	Victim / Offender	34
17.	Choices	36
18.	Dilemmas	38
19.	InXs	40
20.	Soaps	42
21.	'Shopping' Centre	44
22.	Parents' Meeting	45
23.	Leaving Home	46
24.	Who Cares?	48
25.	Child II Adult	50
26.	Retreat - Relationships	52
27.	Celebration of Affirmation	60

1 INTRODUCTIONS

Five interesting things about you...

1.
2.
3.
4.
5.

What are the qualities of a good candidate...

?

Baptism quiz
Answer: T - true; F - false or D - debatable

B - only **b**abies are baptised.
A - **a**ll unbaptised people go to hell.
P - only a **p**riest can baptise.
T - baptism is not a **t**rivial decision.
I - **i**t is necessary to go to Church once you are baptised.
S - in baptism you accept Jesus as **S**aviour.
M - it doesn't **m**atter if you believe in God.

What is Confirmation?

The Church has always considered that baptism is really important. When adults are baptised they are confirmed at the same time because unlike babies, they are able to make a conscious decision to accept Jesus into their lives. When babies and children are baptised, they are baptised on the understanding that their parents and godparents will bring them up as Christians. The parents make the promise on behalf of their children. At Confirmation you take on the responsibility yourself and confirm the promises made for you. Confirmation is an outward sign of *your* personal commitment to Jesus Christ.

Diamond: D - dedication, I - end of Initiation, A - affirming Baptismal promises, M - more understanding, O - obligation, N - new start, discovery

LifeSpan — Reaching Confirmation in the Spirit

The Pyramid of Preparation

How did the ancient Egyptians go about building the great pyramids? No one knows for sure but they certainly put much effort and planning into them. As a result, the pyramids have stood the test of time and they are still admired to this day. The apex of the pyramid stands high only because of the firm and wide base below it, and from the top you get a much better view than from the ground.

Confirmation is the apex of this part of the programme. In order to get to the summit you need to prepare the foundations below. Everything that you will learn will help you appreciate the view from the top. Keep track of your progress through the programme by colouring or shading in the 'chambers' on the pyramid as you pass through them on the course.

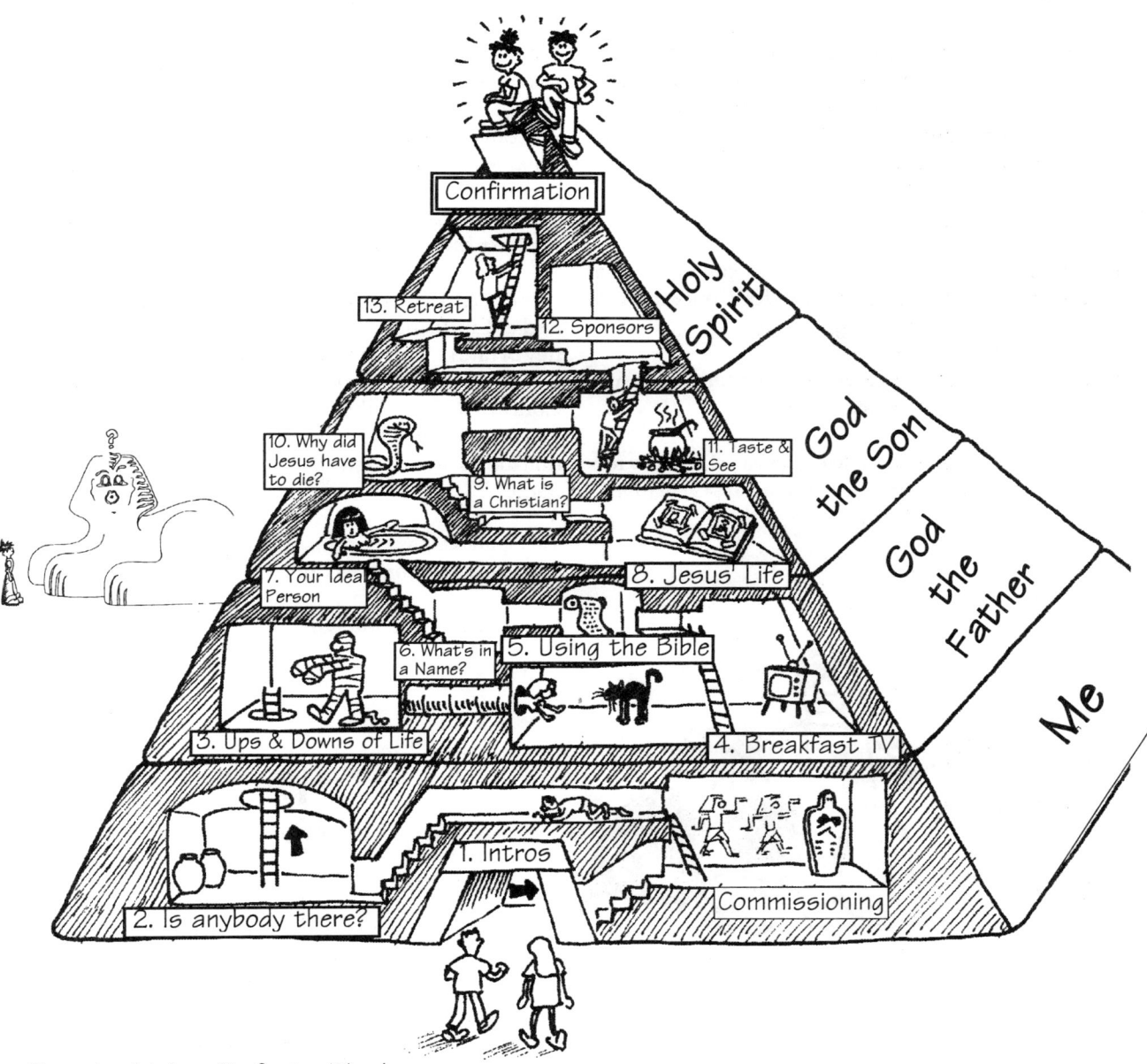

[Pyramid diagram with labelled chambers: Confirmation (apex), 13. Retreat, 12. Sponsors, 10. Why did Jesus have to die?, 9. What is a Christian?, 11. Taste & See, 7. Your Ideal Person, 8. Jesus' Life, 6. What's in a Name?, 5. Using the Bible, 3. Ups & Downs of Life, 4. Breakfast TV, 2. Is anybody there?, 1. Intros, Commissioning. Side faces labelled: Holy Spirit, God the Son, God the Father, Me.]

Practice Makes Perfect - Words

- Be a person who keeps their word & promises.
- If you make an agreement - then stick to it. People will respect you and know where they stand with you.
- Do not enter into promises lightly, but consider your thoughts carefully.
- Do not let others make up your mind for you - but be open to other people's ideas.
- Be a person who keeps the Word of the Lord & lives by His teachings.

CANDIDATE'S BOOK — 1. INTRODUCTIONS — 3

CELEBRATION OF COMMISSIONING

The Order of the Celebration

To commission someone is to give them a special task to perform. This celebration marks the start of the programme and informs the parish that a period of instruction has begun to prepare young people for Confirmation.

Commissioning takes place during Catholic Mass/Anglican Holy Communion in place of, or after, the sermon. The simple form is presented here, but catechists and clergy may want to adapt it to suit their particular parish.

There are three stages involved:

■ commissioning the candidates to stand up and declare their interest in preparing for Confirmation and attending the faith programme,

■ commissioning the catechists/leaders who are going to help the candidates prepare,

■ commissioning the people of the parish to pray for and support the candidates and catechists/leaders.

Commissioning of Candidates

The candidates, parents and catechists sit where they please in the congregation.

The priest calls the candidates forward.

Priest: "I invite those young people who have expressed an interest in joining our Faith Programme to come forward".

The candidates leave their family and come forward to stand in a single line in front of the altar or chancel steps.

The priest/representatives welcome each of them by shaking their hands. Then the priest says:

Priest: "At Baptism you were made a child of God and at Confirmation you will begin your adult journey of faith. As a reminder of your Baptism, and your intention to learn and prepare for the Sacrament of Confirmation and the Rite of Affirmation, please dip your finger into the water, brought from the Baptismal font, touch your forehead and say your Christian name".

The candidates dip their finger in the bowl of (holy) water and touch their foreheads and in turn say:

Candidate: "I was Baptised..................................(N)"

Commissioning of Catechists/Leaders

The priest calls the catechists forward.

Priest: "Will those from the faith community who have agreed to help the candidates on the programme please come forward."

The catechists come forward.

Priest: "Will you help the candidates prepare through prayer and learning to receive the Sacrament of Confirmation?".

Catechists: "We will."

Priest: "Therefore, I empower you on behalf of the faith community in .... (name of parish/church) to guide these young people on the faith programme. Be diligent in your preparation, your learning and your teaching. Never forget to pray for the help of your heavenly Father and the support of your Christian brothers and sisters. May God bless you in this ministry."

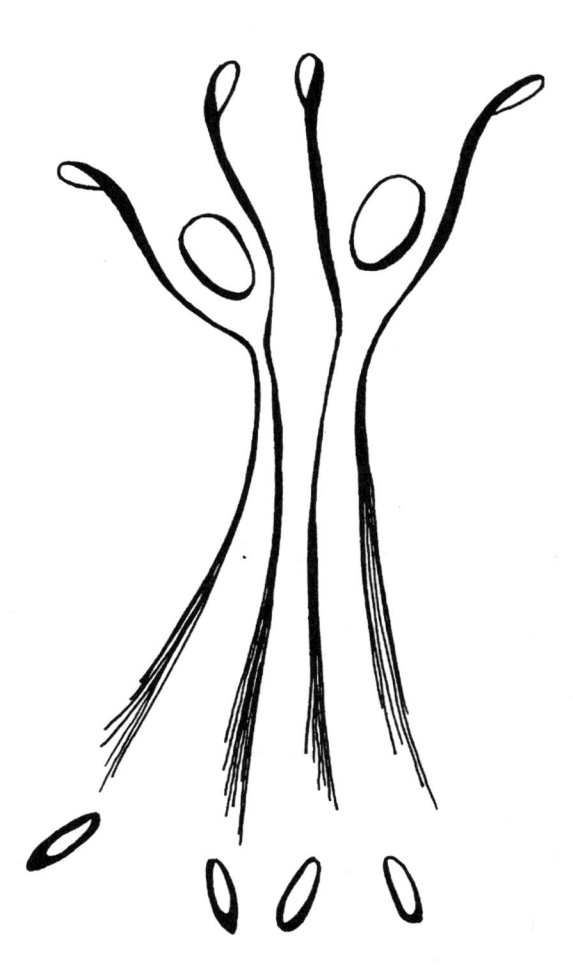

Commissioning of the Faith Community

The priest then addresses the congregation.

Priest: "During this Rite of Commissioning, the catechist(s)/leader(s) have been given the task of guiding these young people or candidates, as they are now called. The candidates also have a duty to learn and prepare for their full reception into the Church.
   As the people of God, we come together to worship God, to witness to His good news and to help each other by encouragement and support. Are you willing to encourage and support these catechists and candidates as they work together on the faith programme?"

Congregation: "We are."

Priest: "I therefore commission you, the faith community of .... (name of church/parish) with the task and duty of praying and supporting the candidates and catechists during the programme."

The catechists lead the candidates to reserved seats where they sit together as a sign that they have been called together as one group.

The Mass/Holy Communion Service continues.

2 Is Anybody There?

Staying in touch

List the different ways people communicate with one another.

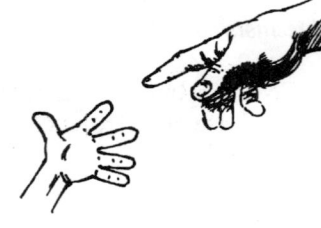

What do people communicate?

Why do people like staying in touch?

Guess What

One form of communication is body-language. You'll be given a card on which is written a message or feeling that you have to communicate - but without speaking or using your hands or any part of your body except your face. The others in the group have to guess what you're trying to communicate. The only word you are allowed to use is 'Yes' when someone has guessed correctly.

Read My Lips

Have you experienced someone wanting to tell you something but they haven't been able to come quite to the point? Perhaps you have been conscious of this yourself. This is an exercise where you have to guess what the person is really talking about. The leader will give you a card and you have to communicate the message but you must not mention the subject directly!

Survey

Carry out a survey:

Ask 3 Christians to list the five most important activities associated with being a Christian.

If you are unable to carry out the survey, write down the 5 activities that you think are important to Christian life.

Five activities associated with Christian life

1. _____
2. _____
3. _____
4. _____
5. _____

LifeSpan — Reaching Confirmation in the Spirit

In what ways does God communicate with us?

Why do we need to keep in contact with God?

In what ways can we communicate with God?

Making Connections

Connect the type of praise to its example; one is already done for you. Which of the various forms of prayer have you experienced?

Praise	Laying on of hands or anointing
Thanksgiving	Song
Dedication	Asking God to help others
Intercession	Grace at meals
Confession	To give into God's hands
Blessing	Saying sorry and asking for God's forgiveness
Meditation	Charity or goodwill
Lament	Asking God to make somebody/thing holy
Action	Quiet time with God
Healing	Expression of sorrow

(Praise — Song)

Practice Makes Perfect - Making Contact

■ Talk to God more often; He is always there, waiting to hear from you. Prayer is not only for church, but is an important part of everyday life, eg pray for help to understand school- or home-work or making difficult decisions.

■ Pray for yourself; thank God for all your 'successes' and ask help for all your 'failures'; ask God to help you be a better person.

■ Pray for other people; your 'enemies' as well as your friends; people who you hear about in the news.

■ Find a regular quiet, regular moment to pray; perhaps, say the Lord's Prayer before going to bed or spend 5 minutes reading the Bible every morning.

3 THE UPS & DOWNS OF LIFE

Have you ever...?

Life is full of ups and downs. Some of the ups and downs you have no control over and they are things that just happen to you. However, there are some that you can control. If you've made fun of someone or belittled them you've not only harmed them but also yourself. You can determine if you're damaging yourself by certain actions you make or decisions you take. This game helps explore these issues. First, just play the game as it is then discuss the deeper meaning behind it. You play the game by throwing the dice (first one to get six starts) and continue as you would 'snakes and ladders'. You move along the same number of squares as the number you get with the roll of the dice. Do whatever the instructions on the square tells you.

Some squares on the board require you to examine your conscience; other squares tell you what you've done, and in others you must answer questions.

Game Board

Downs of Life • Charity • Greed • Envy • Ups & Downs

60 If you've used bad language today, go back 3 spaces.	61	62	63 If you've ever taken something belonging to someone else without them knowing go down the drain pipe.	64
59 Have you helped with the washing up this week? If so go up.	58	57 Have you ganged up on a class mate? If Yes, go back 2 spaces.	56	55
40	41 Have you told a lie today? If so, go back 2 spaces.	42	43	44 If you can name the four Gospels, po-go up 1 level.
39	38	37 Have you ignored people who've made fun of you? Yes - go forward 5.	36	35 If you've ever vandalised anything go back 9 spaces.
20 Have you ever helped someone in need? If Yes go forward 10 spaces.	21	22 Have you ever said a prayer for someone in need? If Yes, go forward 2.	23	24
19	18	17 If you've ever forgiven someone for something horrible done to you rocket up.	16	15 Do you go to Church regularly? If Yes go forward 3 spaces.
Start	1 If you always throw a '1' then go ahead 3 spaces.	2	3 If you've ever stuck up for someone cannon-ball up.	4

Success • Ups & Downs of Life • Failure • Ups & Downs of Life • Winning • Ups &

Love • Ups & Downs of Life • Anger • Ups & Downs of

Discussion points

- Are the events in your life as lucky as a dice roll?
- What sorts of things control what happens in your life?
- Divide your answers into 'positives' and 'negatives'. How might you change the 'negative' ones?
- Is there a way of 'cheating' at this game?

of Life • Meaness • Ups & Downs of Life • Happiness •

65	66	67	68 If you've ever cheated at a board game - go down the rubbish chute.	64 Finish
54 Have you been cheeky to your parents today? If Yes go down the plug-hole.	53	52 If you always get up late in the mornings - miss a go.	51	50
45	46	47	48	49 Have you ever found something belonging to someone else and tried to return it? If Yes climb up.
34 Have you refused to help someone today? If Yes, go back 2 spaces.	33	32 If you care about the environment, God's creation - go up.	31	30 Have you ever made fun of someone in front of others? If Yes - go down with the apple.
25 If you've been well behaved during this game - have another go.	26	27	28 If you don't do your homework until the last minute - go back 2 spaces	29
14	13	12 Have you read the Bible without being made to do so? If Yes, go ahead 2 spaces.	11	10
5 Have you ever done anything charitable? If Yes, what did you do? Rocket up.	6	7 If you were rude to someone today - go back 3 spaces.	8	9

Ups & Downs of Life • Anger • Ups & Downs of Life •

CANDIDATE'S BOOK 3. UPS & DOWNS 9

4 BREAKFAST TV

What this is about...

You're going to put together a programme about **God the Father** in the style of a Breakfast TV show - that other people are going to watch! If your family has a video camera tell the leader as it may come in useful later on!

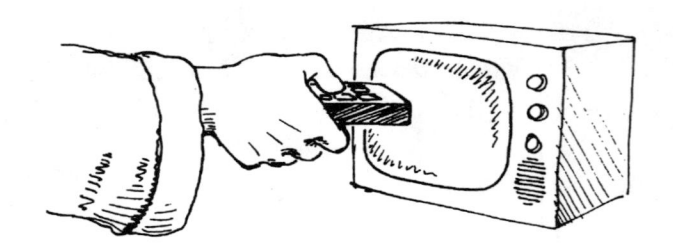

Planning this Breakfast TV programme takes time. This is how you can go about it...

■ Read the instructions given in the Week 1, 2 and 3 boxes.
■ Be guided by the catechist.

Your Notes

Week 1

The catechist/leader will give you instructions. You are all to be TV researchers, writers and presenters. The catechist is the 'programme editor'.

■ Think of all the different items and features that are on a breakfast TV programme. Write them down.

■ When you have a list, ask the editor to give you an assignment.
• The assignment is ....
• Read the Bible references you are given and make notes...

■ Suggestions of how to carry out the assignment. Ask yourself:
1. What is this story about? (ask the 'editor' if you are not sure about the meaning of the reading)
2. Does it mention God anywhere?
3. What is God's role in this story?
4. What is God like in this story, eg friendly, fiercesome, loving etc.

■ Now see if you can write your item for Breakfast TV based on the story. Make it interesting for someone who might be 'watching' the show.

An example...

Your Notes

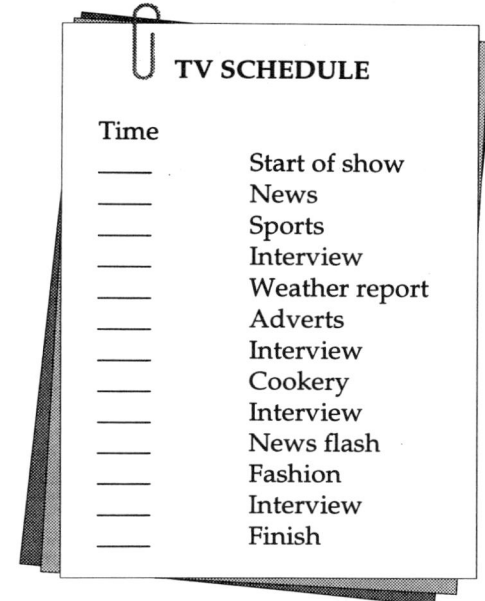

TV SCHEDULE

Time	
___	Start of show
___	News
___	Sports
___	Interview
___	Weather report
___	Adverts
___	Interview
___	Cookery
___	Interview
___	News flash
___	Fashion
___	Interview
___	Finish

Week 2

Put the various assignments together and construct the TV show.

■ If you have not already done so, then think up the name of the TV station and of the show.

■ Link together the assignments to produce an interesting show. Time how long various assignments take and come up with a schedule. Look at the example TV schedule but do not feel you have to follow it exactly.

■ Avoid having similar items one after the other. Have the 'features' (for example, the weather, sport, cookery etc) in between the more serious articles.

■ Decide how long the show is going to last. If you have too many items you must decide which ones to remove. TV producers need to be ruthless!

Week 3

This week is the complete run through. Decide who you would like to invite to see the show: parents, friends, some elderly people etc. If everything goes well, consider putting the show on during a Mass or Service to the congregation. If anyone has use of a camcorder then the show could be recorded on video and the video shown to groups in the parish. If you can make copies of the video then everyone can have a copy as a souvenir.

Practice Makes Perfect - God and Me...

There comes a point in everyone's life when they have to make a commitment. Read the story of Abraham's covenant with God in Gen 15. This is a real turning point for Abraham when he and God make promises to each other.

Confirmation is our version of a promise or 'covenant'. Make a list of promises you might make between you and God in your Confirmation.

My promises to God	God's promises to me

CANDIDATE'S BOOK   4. BREAKFAST TV

5 BIBLE-BASHING

Prayer
Dear Lord, today we will be thinking about your book, *the Book*, the Bible! Give us: faith to believe what is good and true; understanding where there is difficulty, and courage to put into practice the Gospel of our Lord Jesus Christ. Amen.

Learning about God.
Write down the ways that we can find out about God.

The Word
For Christians, a major source of knowledge about God is The Book - The Holy Bible. In our lives, we are surrounded by books, school textbooks, exercise books, newspapers, comics and other printed matter.

Think about the following items and their principal uses; then try to fill in the table, writing in the similarities and dissimilarities of each compared with the Bible.

- Bible 
- Cookery book
- Manual 
- Comics
- Newspapers...
- Maps
- Biography

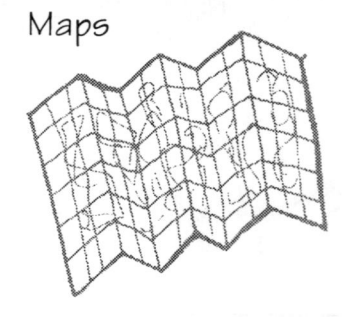

Item	Similarity to Bible	Dissimilarity to Bible
Map		
Manual		
Newspaper		
Biography		
Cookery Book		

A Thought

The Bible is an important book for Christians. But Christianity is not based solely on a book but on a person - Jesus Christ - the Word of God. The Bible is valued because of its Good News of a loving Father, His only Son and His Spirit, living in the world today.

The Bible is the home...

...of the stories of the early people of God. Using your Bible, try to answer these questions:

1. What are the two major parts of the Bible called?
2. In which Book of the Bible do Adam and Eve appear?
3. Name one Book of the Bible that is named after a man.
4. Name one Book of the Bible that is named after a woman.
5. Which Book of the Bible sounds like royalty?
6. What are the names of the four Gospel writers?
7. Name two people who wrote 'letters' in the New Testament.

Practice Makes Perfect - 'Dusting' down your Bible.

■ At home, find where your family Bible is kept, and place it in a more prominent place or keep it near your bed.

■ Do not try to read the Bible from start to finish; find a book in your local religious bookshop which helps you understand readings from the Bible; ask the bookshop assistant to help you find one. Read parts of the Bible with friends or family and share what you all understand from the reading.

6 What's in a Name?

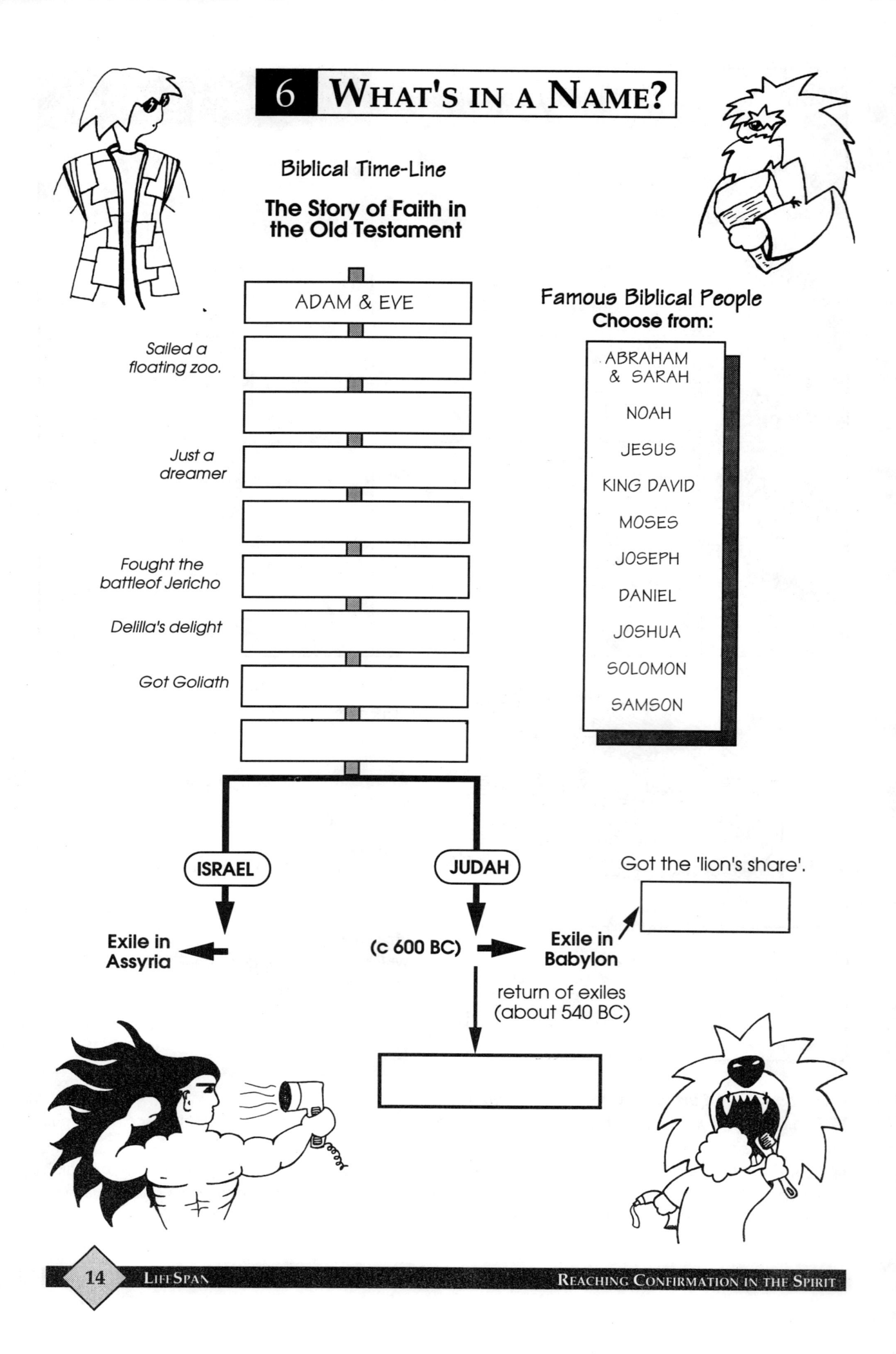

Biblical Time-Line
The Story of Faith in the Old Testament

ADAM & EVE

Sailed a floating zoo.

Just a dreamer

Fought the battle of Jericho

Delilla's delight

Got Goliath

ISRAEL   JUDAH

Famous Biblical People
Choose from:

- ABRAHAM & SARAH
- NOAH
- JESUS
- KING DAVID
- MOSES
- JOSEPH
- DANIEL
- JOSHUA
- SOLOMON
- SAMSON

Got the 'lion's share'.

Exile in Assyria

(c 600 BC) → **Exile in Babylon**

return of exiles (about 540 BC)

14 LifeSpan — Reaching Confirmation in the Spirit

Family Tree

How much of your family's history do you know? See if you can construct your own family tree. Start at the top 'branches' and put in the names of your living relatives. Work towards the 'roots' writing in previous generations of relatives as far back as you can remember.

When you do this exercise you will probably find it hard to remember the names of your ancestors. In Biblical times this was not so difficult. People were generally illiterate so they put much effort in memorising their family's history. New members of the family were told stories about their ancestors.

The Old and New Testaments form a record of a 'family' of people that shared a faith in God - a 'faith family'. In baptism, you became a member of this faith family. In Confirmation, you are invited to acknowledge that you want to continue as a member of this family. The stories in the Bible are not about remote and ancient people - but are about our previous family members.

My Faith Story

Drawn below is a time-line which represents your life. The clock at the start of the line began ticking when you came into the world and the end of the line is where you are now. Along the line, write in those significant or special events in your life. After you have done that, try to identify times when God has been present in a special way.

Now

CANDIDATE'S BOOK 6. WHAT'S IN A NAME? 15

7 YOUR IDEAL PERSON

Imagine for a moment your idea of the ideal or perfect person

What clothes does he/she wear?
Glamorous clothes, sporty gear, trendy clothes?

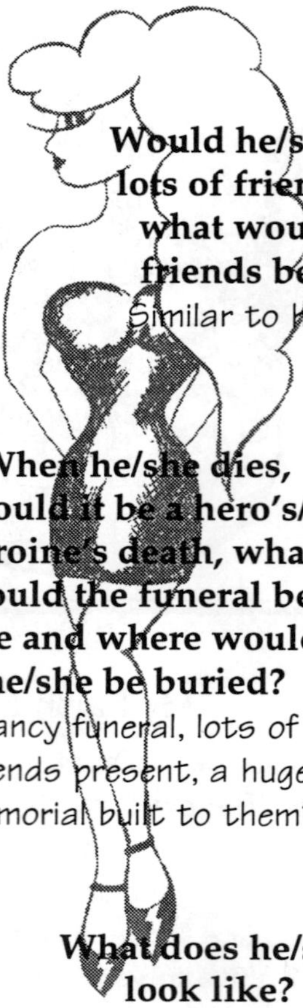

What sort of job does he/she do?
Fashion model, racing driver, brain surgeon, artist, pop singer?

What sort of car does he/she drive?
A Porsche, Skoda?

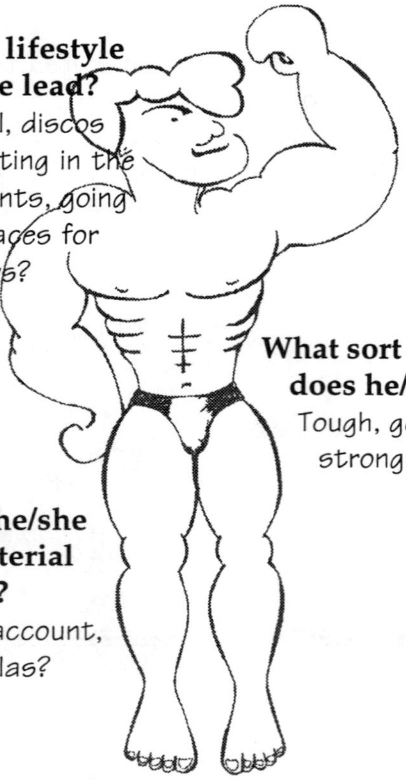

What sort of lifestyle does he/she lead?
Party animal, discos most night, eating in the best restaurants, going to exotic places for holidays?

What sort of character does he/she have?
Tough, gentle, kind, strong-minded?

What does he/she own in material goods?
A large bank account, yachts, villas?

What sort of house does he/she live in?
A mansion, with swimming pools etc?

Would he/she have lots of friends and what would the friends be like?
Similar to him/her?

When he/she dies, would it be a hero's/heroine's death, what would the funeral be like and where would he/she be buried?
Fancy funeral, lots of friends present, a huge memorial built to them?

What does he/she look like?
- handsome/pretty?
- colour of eyes, hair?
- slim/muscular/athletic?

Would you want to be this 'ideal person'?

If so, why?

If not, why not?

What might be the pitfalls of leading a life like that of your ideal person? What are the benefits?

Why do people often want to be like someone else?

---

16 LifeSpan   Reaching Confirmation in the Spirit

Jesus as my ideal

What sort of clothes did He wear?

What sort of house did He live in?

What sort of job did He have?

What sort of friends did He have?

What did Jesus look like?

What sort of lifestyle did He lead?

When Jesus died what sort of funeral did He have?

What sort of character did Jesus have?

Did He own much material goods?

What sort of transport did He have?

Would you want to be like Jesus?

If so, why?

If not, why not?

What might be the pitfalls of being and acting like Jesus?

Practice Makes Perfect - What is Important?

■ Re-evaluate what is important in your life.

■ Think about what is short-lived and gives happiness for an instant, as opposed to things that have value for a long time.

■ Think about what builds you up as a person, and gives you strength to get through ordeals and upsets.

■ Pray to Jesus to help you make the right decisions in life.

Jesus, I accept You into my life...

'Dear Jesus, I would like you to be my friend. Please come into my life today and help me to live as You want me to. Amen.'

CANDIDATE'S BOOK

7. YOUR IDEAL PERSON   17

8 Jesus' Life

TRUE / FALSE?

1. Jesus was Jewish?
2. Jesus was an only child?
3. Jesus lived in Bethlehem until He was 30 years old?
4. Jesus' home was in Capernaum?
5. Jesus preached most of the time in Jerusalem?
6. Jesus threatened to destroy the Temple and rebuild it in 3 days?
7. Jesus overturned tables and disrupted trade in the Temple courts?
8. Jesus said that He could forgive people their sins?
9. Everybody knew that Jesus was the Jewish Messiah?
10. Jesus wanted to start a new religion?
11. At His trial Jesus was found guilty of starting a revolution?
12. Jesus' death was a tragic end to a promising lifetime of serving God's people?

What did people in the New Testament say about Jesus?

Read the Bible texts and summarise what is said.

Mark 2: 1-12

Mark 3: 20-22

Mark 8: 27-30

What does the average man and the woman in the street say about Jesus ...?

Priest

Comforter   Healer   Son of God

Saviour

Liberator

Prophet   King   Friend

Protector

Peacemaker

Messiah

What do you say?

Practice Makes Perfect - Hurting with words.

■ Speech can be used for good or ill. Do not use God's gift of speech to bring people down, to ruin their reputation, to spread rumour or gossip.

■ Use speech as God intended: for us to get to know one another, to tell the truth and to spread God's message to others.

■ Do not use God or Jesus' name in bad language; try to avoid swearing; find other words to express your feelings.

9 WHAT MAKES A CHRISTIAN?

Does this make me a Christian?

I go to church every Sunday. ☐

I believe in God. ☐

I try my best to do what is right. ☐

I believe in helping others. ☐

I was born in a Christian country. ☐

My parents are Christian. ☐

**Tell-tale Signs.
How can you tell...?**

...what someone is and what they stand for?

Jesus said (Mark 1:14,15; Mark 8:34,35; John 3:5,6)

The first Christians said (Acts 2:37-39)

Our Baptism service says:

20 LifeSpan — Reaching Confirmation in the Spirit

North

1

2   5

South

Candidate's Book   9. What makes a Christian?   21

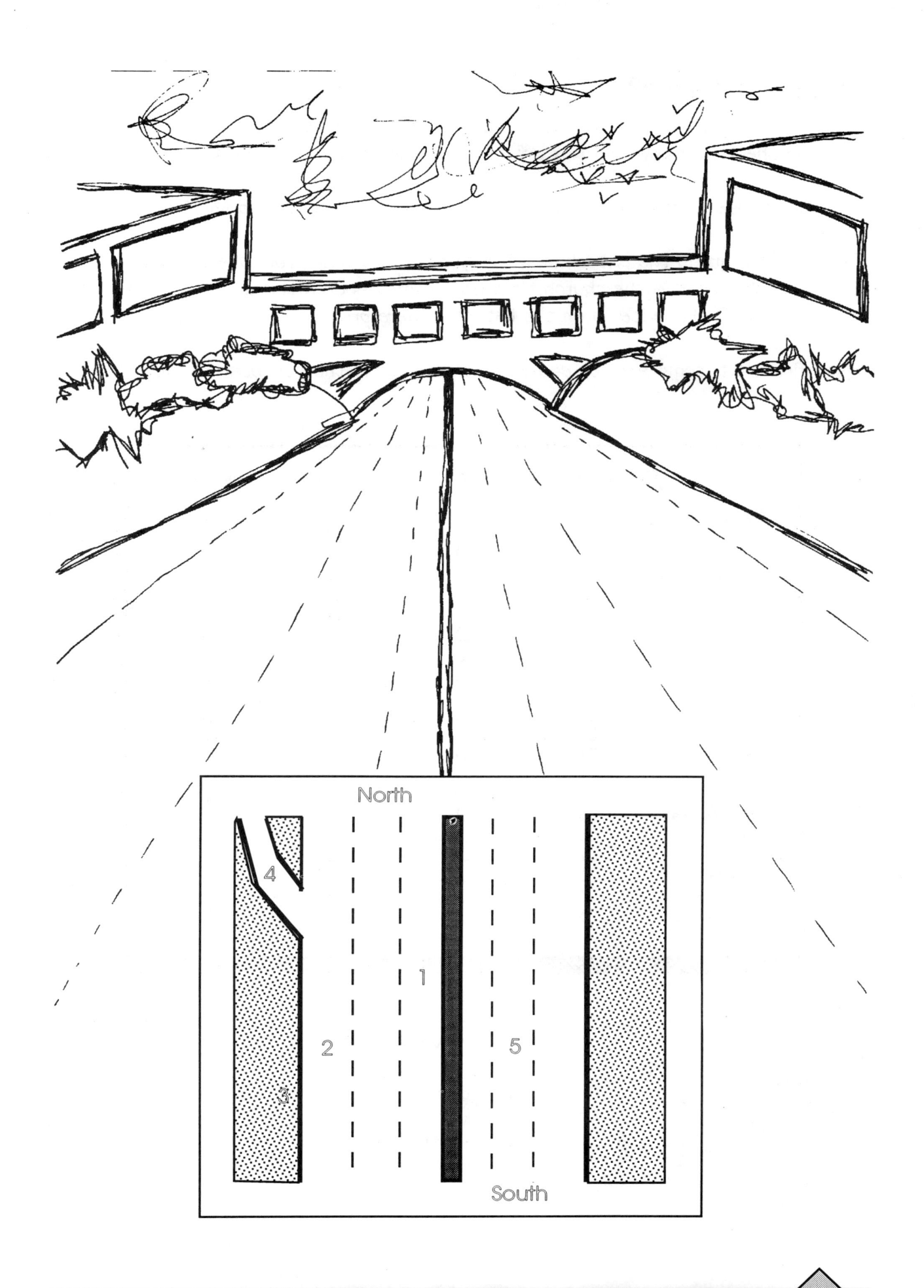

What is Church?

What makes up a church? Wander around a Roman Catholic and an Anglican church with the checklist below and tick off all the items that you can spot.

Then tick those items which you think are absolutely essential to the Church.

Finally, in the group the catechist will read some extracts from the Bible about the Early Church - that is the church that was formed soon after Jesus ascended into Heaven. Tick off those items on the list which were present in the Early Church.

If you find that items are not essential, then what is their purpose in the Church today?

	Roman Catholic	Anglican	Essential	Early Church
Building	❑	❑	❑	❑
Font	❑	❑	❑	❑
Altar	❑	❑	❑	❑
Candles	❑	❑	❑	❑
Pulpit	❑	❑	❑	❑
Pews	❑	❑	❑	❑
Stain-glass windows	❑	❑	❑	❑
Cross	❑	❑	❑	❑
Tabernacle	❑	❑	❑	❑
Statues	❑	❑	❑	❑
Vestry	❑	❑	❑	❑
Organ	❑	❑	❑	❑
Sacristy	❑	❑	❑	❑
Choir	❑	❑	❑	❑
Robes	❑	❑	❑	❑
Altar servers	❑	❑	❑	❑
Priest	❑	❑	❑	❑
People	❑	❑	❑	❑
Accolytes	❑	❑	❑	❑
Poor boxes	❑	❑	❑	❑
Parish newsletter	❑	❑	❑	❑

Practice Makes Perfect - Following Jesus.

■ At Baptism, you became a Christian unknowingly.

■ At Confirmation, you will be declaring that you are making the decision to be a follower of Christ.

■ Accept your Christianity and become more responsible for your actions in the Church and life.

In the previous exercise, you were looking for items that were plainly visible in the Church. There are 'items' that cannot be seen when wandering around a church building and some of these are listed below. Go through the list and write down what you think their purpose is and how we know they are there since we can't see them.

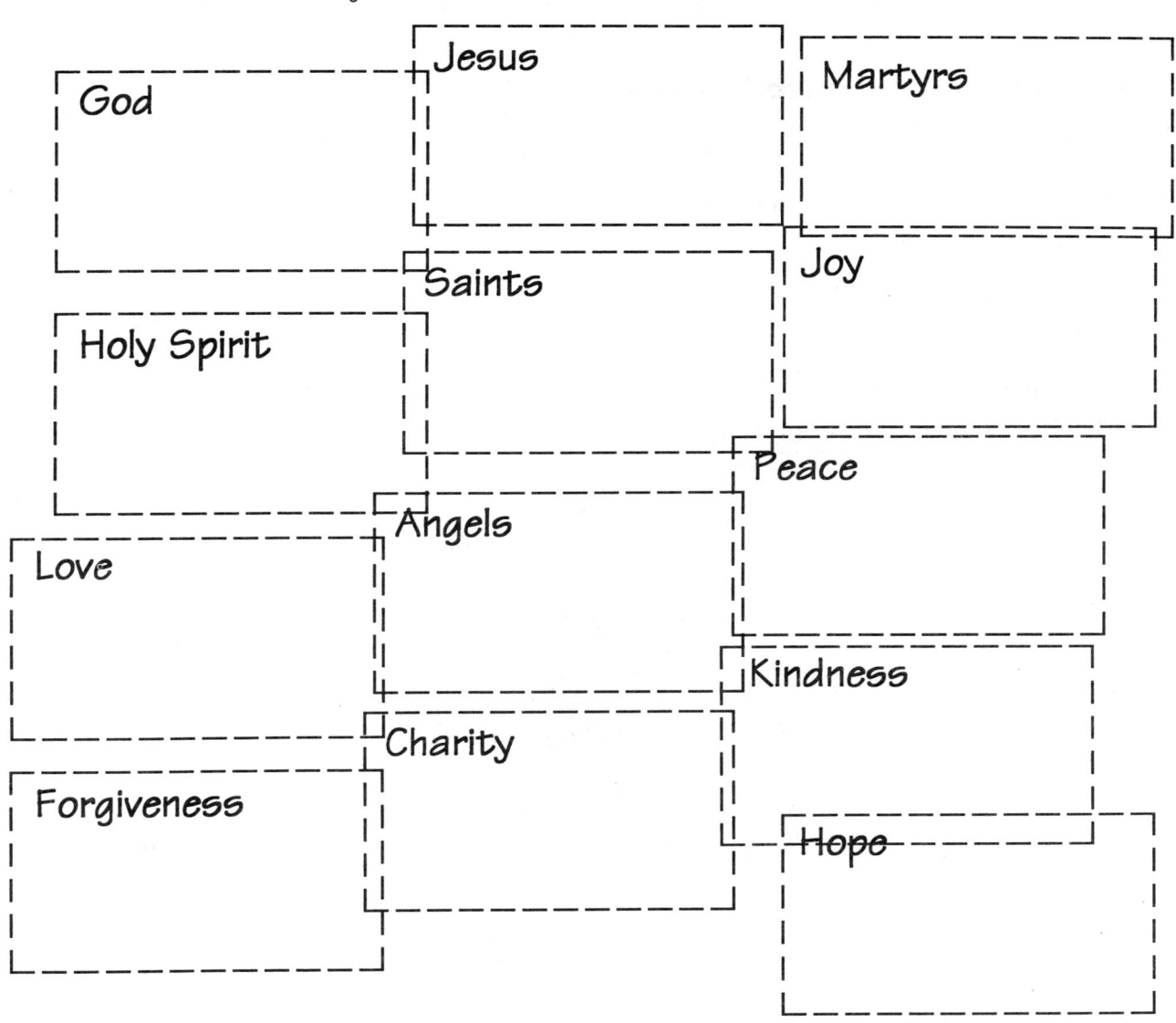

- God
- Jesus
- Martyrs
- Saints
- Joy
- Holy Spirit
- Peace
- Angels
- Love
- Kindness
- Charity
- Forgiveness
- Hope

Private Eye
Imagine that you are a private detective in the times of the Roman Empire. The Roman authorities want to close down the Christian Church. They come to you to find out what 'charges' they can put against the Church. Do some detective work by looking through Acts in the New Testament and make a list of the sorts of charges that the Romans can bring.

Either...

Or...

'Selling' the Church
Imagine your group is putting together a brochure to attract young people to your church. Put together some ideas of why young people should attend church.

Or...

Making Changes
Make a list of the differences and similarities of your church and the Early Church. What would you change or keep the same in your church if you had the power to make changes. How could you go about making any changes?

CANDIDATE'S BOOK — 9. WHAT MAKES A CHRISTIAN? — 23

10 — WHY DID JESUS HAVE TO DIE?

I. SIN BIN

What do you think about people in general?

Put a tick by one of the statements given below

People are basically GOOD, though capable of being bad.	☐
People are basically BAD, though capable of being good.	☐
People are basically NEUTRAL, and are shaped by their surroundings & upbringing.	☐

How good are you at ...

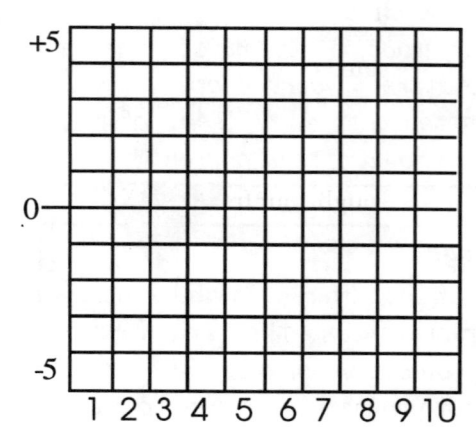

(graph: x-axis 1–10, y-axis −5 to +5)

1. sport
2. maths
3. reading
4. being on time
5. doing what your parents say
6. doing homework on time
7. computer games
8. being nice to people
9. dancing
10. singing

Practice Makes Perfect - Accepting yourself.

■ Be positive about yourself. There might be things you don't like about yourself. Recognising what might be wrong is the first step to putting it right!

■ Jesus recognised sin in the world - and He conquered it by sacrificing Himself for us.

■ Ask Jesus to forgive your wrongs and to help you be a better person.

LifeSpan — Reaching Confirmation in the Spirit

II. Saviour

Why was Jesus killed?

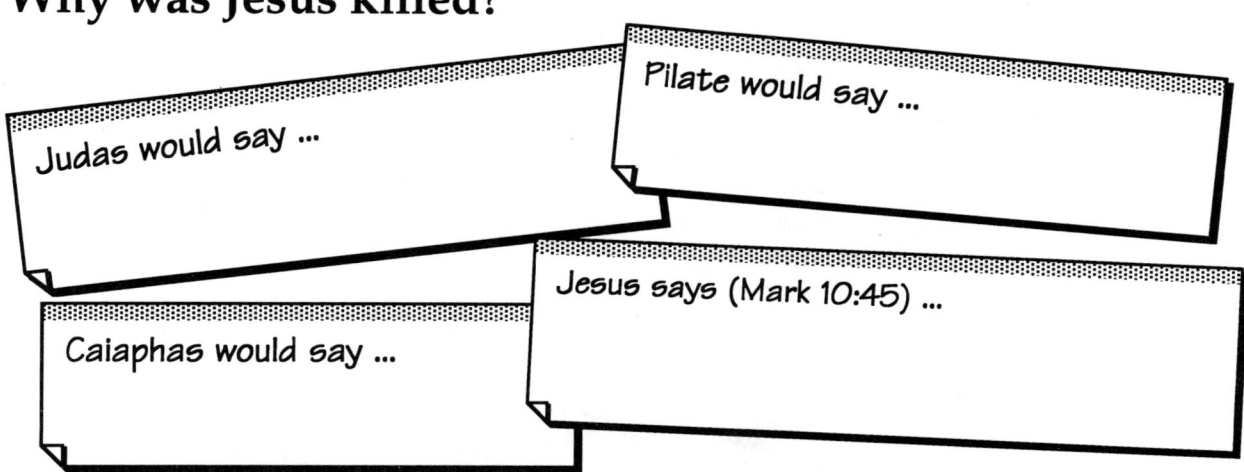

Judas would say ...

Pilate would say ...

Caiaphas would say ...

Jesus says (Mark 10:45) ...

Role play

- Work in pairs...
- One person has to describe to another why Jesus died...
- However, one of you comes from a South Sea island and the other is an Eskimo and you can't speak each other's language...
- You have to find a way of communicating with each other.

S.A.V.I.O.U.R.

S - sacrifice: Jesus was offered as a sacrifice to atone for sin - Jn 1:29; 1 Pet 1:19.

A - acquittal: Jesus took the blame for our sins to set us free - Isa 53:5, 11.

V - victory: Jesus' apparent failure on the cross was turned into victory over evil - Matt 5:39-42; 1 Pet 3:1.

I - identify: Jesus identified with us; we follow His example - 1 Pet 2:21; Rom 5:7-8.

O - only once: We no longer have to make animal sacrifices as Jesus was a sacrifice for us - Heb 10:1-18.

U - undying: Jesus rose on Easter Sunday; Christians believe He defeated death and now enables all who believe and trust in Him to have everlasting life. Matt 28:1-15.

R - Ransom: Jesus 'bought' our freedom from sin - 1 Pet 1:18-19.

Activity:

Produce a display for your church to explain in simple terms what the above actually means. Alternatively, produce small sketches or dramas to put these into everyday terms.

11 TASTE & SEE

Welcome to the celebration of a meal. This meal is an enactment of the Passover meal celebrated by the Jewish people at the time of Jesus. Depending on how your catechist or leader has organised the session, there might be an opportunity for you to 'taste and see' how this ancient meal was celebrated.

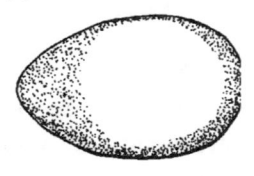

wine goblet

boiled egg

26 LifeSpan — Reaching Confirmation in the Spirit

lamb stew

parsley

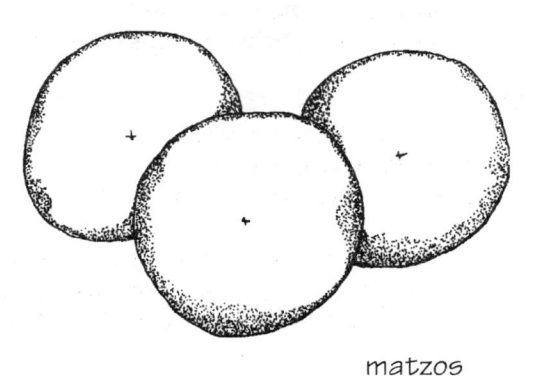

matzos

bitter herbs, sweet herbs and salt water

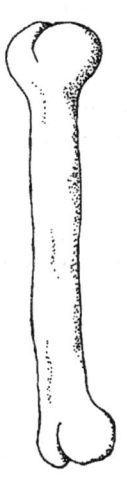

shank-bone

12 SPONSOR CHECKLIST

You will shortly need to decide about sponsor(s) for Confirmation. To help you decide here is a checklist. Tick the box if the statement applies. If there are lots of ticks then that person is a good choice.

Tick if YES.

- ☐ Is the choice of sponsor yours? Parents and family can help you decide but the final say should be your's alone.

Proposed sponsor(s) _____ , _____

Is he/she:
- ☐ Catholic / Anglican? (depending on your denomination)
- ☐ Confirmed?
- ☐ someone who would be prepared to pray for you?
- ☐ someone you can confide in about a problem with your faith?

Does he/she:
- ☐ attend Mass / Holy Communion regularly? (depending on your denomination)
- ☐ encourage you in the faith?
- ☐ have a living belief in Jesus Christ?

Do you:
- ☐ trust and like this person?
- ☐ see them regularly?
- ☐ respect his/her views?

Ask the person you have chosen if he/she would be happy to be your sponsor. Before he/she makes up their mind show them the checklist below.
If there are lots of ticks then he/she would make a good sponsor.

Sponsor, please read the following checklist and tick if Yes.

Proposed candidate: _____

Are you:
- ☐ Catholic / Anglican? (depending on your denomination)
- ☐ Confirmed?
- ☐ a person that the candidate can confide in?

Do you:
- ☐ attend Mass / Holy Communion regularly? (depending on your denomination)
- ☐ have a living belief in Jesus Christ?

Would you:
- ☐ be prepared to pray for him/her ?
- ☐ encourage the candidate in the faith?

Does the candidate:
- ☐ trust and like you?
- ☐ see you regularly?
- ☐ respect your views?

Thank you for your cooperation.

13 CONNECTIONS WITH THE SPIRIT

During this programme you have been exploring God the Father and God the Son in your life and in the life of the Church. However, a very important aspect of Confirmation is the role played by God the Holy Spirit. This is so important that a special time has been put aside for the group to learn more about the Holy Spirit. The catechist will arrange for the group to work together over a weekend either in your home parish, or you might all go away together for one day or a weekend. Your catechist will give you all the details in due course. It is very important that you attend because you will then understand better the Sacrament or Sign of Confirmation.

At your Confirmation there will be a special visitor - the Bishop. One of his many roles in your local church is to Confirm candidates. Some of his responsibilities are given below. See if you can add to the list by asking your parish priest - or perhaps asking the Bishop himself.

Shepherd of the Flock...

Church leader...

Guardian of the Faith...

'Descended' from St Peter...

...Ordains deacons & priests

...Looks after a diocese

...Confirms Christians

CANDIDATE'S BOOK 13. CONNECTIONS WITH THE SPIRIT 29

14 OVERVIEW

COMING OF AGE IN THE SPIRIT

Coming of Age in the Spirit is the second part of the
LifeSpan Faith Programme for young Christians.
It is intended for young people who have been recently Confirmed.
This part may run immediately after Reaching Confirmation in the Spirit
or after a short gap.
Your catechist or parish priest will tell you how it will be run.

17. Choices.
The possible consequences of making decisions.

16. Victim-offender.
Offence causes suffering.

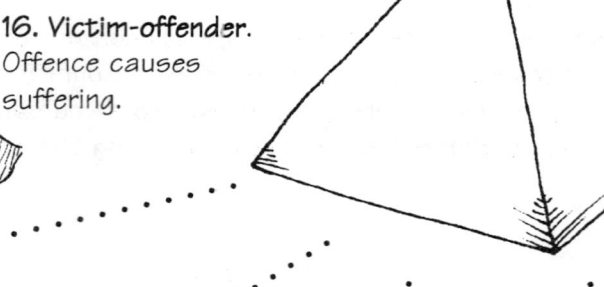

14. Overview of Coming of Age in the Spirit

15. Doubt.
What it means to doubt yourself and God.

21. 'Shopping' centre.
Discovering the true meaning of loyalty

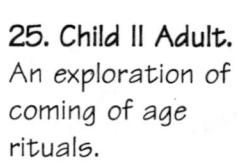

25. Child II Adult.
An exploration of coming of age rituals.

LifeSpan — Coming of Age in the Spirit

20. Soaps.
Examining topical issues through role-play.

19. InXs
The effects of doing things to excess.

23. Leaving home.
An enactment of a drama and the issues raised.

22. Parents' meeting.
What it means to be a parent.

24. Who cares?
Responding to a plea for help.

18. Dilemmas.
A game of moral dilemmas.

27. Rite of Affirmation.
The concluding celebration of Coming of Age in the Spirit.

26. Relationships.
A weekend retreat.

CANDIDATE'S BOOK — 14. OVERVIEW — 31

15 DOUBT?

There are times in life when we feel unsure of ourselves and doubt our ability to cope with events. At times like these we become unsure of ourself and even doubt others. These tend to be times when we are faced with change; change of circumstances and/or opportunities to change ourself as we grow up to become what is often referred as an 'adult'. We may then even distrust our faith.

Peter is 18 years old and about to enter university. His application was sent, he has been interviewed and now awaits 'the letter' which will tell him whether he has been accepted or not. The wait is proving difficult for him.

Peter is at the moment alone in his room dealing with his incredulity. He is lying on his bed. The tape he was listening to is over. The house is quiet, as everyone is either at school or at work. He is battling with his two 'selfs' and he is desperately trying to be 'reasonable' as his parents often tell him to be at times like this.

Peter is coming to a crossroads in his life and in the quiet of his bedroom he is debating with his positive self (Person 1) and his negative self (Person 2), both of whom are perched either side of his headboard! Person 1 is frowning and grouchy in appearance, Person 2 displays joy of life and wears a smile projecting confidence and enthusiasm.

Peter: I knew I wouldn't make it. There's no way I can be what they expect of me. I'm just not good enough. Uni; that's for intelligent people, not for me, is it?

Person 1: You're not clever enough, you couldn't cope with such levels of learning.

Person 2: (to Person 1) Of course he can. What are you talking about?

Person 1: (to Person 2) Can't you see how low he feels about the situation? He just can't do it.

Person 2: Just imagine, Peter. You make it there, meet new people, make new friends and a whole new world is opened to you.

Peter: But they haven't written to me yet. Some of my friends already know they have a place. I knew all along I wasn't good enough.

Person 1: (looking at Person 2) See the lad knows. He's quite right. He should stay here where he feels at home and settle for the first job he can get. He'll be alright.

Person 2: (laughing at the prospect) Peter, can you imagine all the things you'd miss, all the opportunities. You would be limiting yourself by staying here. Your parents are right; you have what it takes, and if you stay here moping you'll lose out.

Peter: What do they know? Parents grew up in a different era, they don't understand. Life was different when they were young.

Person 1: Quite right. on another planet even...

Peter: (suddenly sits up and faces the headboard) Now hold on, they're not that bad surely. That's my parents you're going on about.

Person 2: (nodding in approval) That's quite correct Peter. Your parents do know - some things don't change with time.

Person 1: (facing Person 2) Why don't you mind your own business. Peter knows his parents and he knows what he can and can't do, and this he can't. Leave him alone if he wants to stay here where he feels safe and at home. What's wrong with that?

Person 2: Peter likes to enjoy life and learn; he has a good memory and he's bright enough to understand and he wants to make things work in life. Does he want to be safe and at home or does he want to be out there in the world where he can grow and enjoy life? Come on Peter, tell us.

Peter: (holding his head in his hands) Oh, I don't know any more; I want to go to Uni but feel I'm not good enough. I want to believe my parents and at the same time I feel inadequate. But then again, what do those interviewers know? They've only met me once for 20 minutes. They don't know anything, any of them. (Peter buries his head under his pillows.)

Person 1: (frowning at Person 2) Now look what you've done. He won't even talk to us now.

Person 2: No, Peter is perfectly correct when he says the interviewers don't know him. They know the person Peter presented to them on the day of the interview and, if Peter - as I know he is capable of - has presented his best, that's what they'll judge him on. But, if they could see him now, well...

(There is a thud somewhere in the house)

Person 1: What's that noise?

Peter: (suddenly sits up) What noise?

Person 2: It could be the postman.

Peter rushes out of the room to check. Collects from the door-mat a letter addressed to him. It's from the University. Peter returns to his room holding the letter.

Peter: Oh God, please help. I can't open this. It's a refusal - I can feel it.

Person 2: Well, unless you open it you won't know.

Person 1: Don't bother Peter. Get a job and stay put. You know you can do that.

Person 2: If you don't open it you'll never know.

Peter opens the letter with hesitation and Person 1 leaves feeling he has lost and Person 2 stays with a grin on his face.

Discuss what Peter has experienced and decide the ending.

What are the possibilities?

What are the real reasons why Peter is doubting himself?

Have you ever felt like Peter about other uncertainties?

Why? What happened?

Many people think that it is wrong to doubt. Is doubt a sin? Why or why not?

Write a play similar to that about Peter, but this time imagine that Peter is debating with himself Does God exist and if He does, then does He help me?' Have two characters (Person 1 and Person 2 again or any other characters) debating each side of the argument.

What practical things can you do when you experience doubt?

Practice Makes Perfect - Beyond a reasonable doubt.

■ Doubting is a natural part of human nature.

■ Doubting involves considering positive points as well as the negative ones.

■ If you feel dragged down by your negative side, remember that you also have a positive side and try to give this more of a hearing.

■ A lot of negative things are said about religion nowadays. Try to balance these things with a more positive outlook. Learn and read about the Bible yourself.

■ Ask Jesus to help you to come to terms with those matters you doubt most.

16 Victim - Offender

Things that can cause you hurt...

being taken for granted...

...being made fun of

bullied...

...things stolen from you

...losing at games to someone who cheated

unappreciated by parents...

...unrewarded for hard work

Hit List

name	offence	punishment
_____	_____	_____
_____	_____	_____
_____	_____	_____
_____	_____	_____

Hit List

name	offence	punishment
_____	_____	_____
_____	_____	_____
_____	_____	_____
_____	_____	_____

LifeSpan — Coming of Age in the Spirit

Times when Jesus was a victim of people's hurts...

- being trapped into making mistakes (Mark 12:13-17);
- being exploited for His powers (Mark 10:35-41);
- being betrayed (Luke 22:1-3, 21-23; Mark 14:42-46);
- having an unfair trial (Mark 14:53-65; Mark 15:1-15);
- being crucifed as a criminal (Luke 23:32-33);
- being born in a stable (Luke 2:1-7);
- being gossiped about (Matt 27:1-2);
- abilities and identity doubted: by Thomas (Jn 20:24-31)
    by His own people (Mark 6:1-6);
- being beaten up (Mark 15:15);
- being spat upon (Matt 26:67);
- being ridiculed (Mark 15:16-20, 29-32);
- clothes stolen and gambled for (Jn 19:23-25);
- being denied (Jn 18:15-27).

For each of these hurts of Jesus...

What would you feel like?

What would you do to the 'offenders' if you had Jesus' power?

What do you think Jesus felt like?

How did Jesus react to the hurts?

If you were to follow Jesus' example...

...how would you now change the hit list for the people who have hurt you?

Practice Makes Perfect - How to treat others.

■ Treat other people as you would want to be treated yourself. Don't have one standard for yourself and another for everyone else.

■ Do onto others as you would have them do unto you.

■ Ask Jesus to help you deal with hurts and difficulties.

17 CHOICES

Freedom ... at a price

Everyone wants to be free - free to do 'their own thing' and to think what they like. With freedom, however, comes responsibility; as your actions and thoughts can affect not only the rest of your life, but also the lives of others.

Freedom to make decisions and responsibility are linked because they result in consequences. These consequences can be short-term (ie affecting you immediately) or long term (ie has an eventual effect on you).

Before looking at your own life, think about the decisions made by people in the Bible.

What happened and what might have happened?

One of the earliest recorded people who had to make a decision was Adam, "Should I eat of the apple?". He knew he shouldn't - but the temptation was too great. Adam answered 'yes' to this question. The short-term effects were that he and Eve were banished from Paradise, the Garden of Eden, and had to work hard the rest of their lives. As we are all descended from Adam and Eve, the long-term effects are that we also have to work and cannot enjoy living in paradise here on Earth. If Adam had said 'no' then they wouldn't have been banished and we might now be enjoying the Garden of Eden.

For each of the Bible references, find out what decisions were made and their consequences and speculate on what might have happened if a different decision was made.

Long-term Effects

Yes

No

Short-term Effects

Yes

No

Should I eat the apple?

LifeSpan — Coming of Age in the Spirit

1. Individuals in the Bible who made decisions.

- Cain (Gen 4:1-8). Should I kill my brother Abel?
- Noah (Gen 6:13-22). Should I build a boat in-land and in dry weather?
- Abraham (Gen 22:1-18). Should I sacrifice my son Isaac?
- Moses (Ex 3:7-12). Should I stand firm against the Pharaoh?
- Ruth (Ruth 1:1-22). Should I remain in my home country or go with my mother-in-law to a foreign land?
- David (1 Sam 16:17; 2 Sam 5:11) - (here, be guided by the catechist).
- Solomon (1 Kings 3:3 to 11:7). Should I choose wisdom or wealth?
- Joseph (Gen 37-50; the catechist will tell you which parts of the text to read). Should I take revenge on my brothers?
- Mary, Mother of Jesus (Lk 1:26-55; 2:34,35, 41-52). Should I accept the angel's demands?
- The rich aristocrat (Lk 18:18-23). Should I give up all my wealth and follow Jesus?
- Jesus (Lk 22:39-44). Should I allow myself to be crucified?

2. Consequences of group decision-making in the Bible.

Now consider people in the Bible who made group decisions.

■ Groups in the Bible that made decisions:
- crowd at Jesus' trial calling to crucify Him (Lk 23:13-25),
- Joseph's brothers ganging up to get rid of him (Gen 37:12-25),
- worship of the golden calf by the Israelites (Ex 32:1-10).

3. Consequences of your decision-making.

Think about your own life and draw out the long and short term effects of doing the following:
- temptation to steal
- 'bunking off' school
- telling lies
- taking drugs
- going to church
- praying

Can you think of other similar actions?

> **Discussion point**
>
> How much does being part of a group affect your decision making?
> If all your friends stopped going to church would that affect your decision to stop going as well?
> Are you a 'free-thinker' or a 'lemming'?

4. Consequences of a group's decision-making in society today.

Consider the long and short term effects of group or gang action in the following activities:
- sending someone 'to Coventry',
- 'playing up' in lessons,
- picking on someone in the playground,
- bullying,
- doing a community project,
- joyriding.

Practice Makes Perfect - The choice is yours.

■ Think through your choices very carefully.

■ Don't just follow the crowd in order to 'fit in'. Think of people who you admire. Are they 'sheep' who follow others blindly?

■ Do what you think is right - not just what is popular.

18 Dilemmas

- The Game -

Introduction to the game

Dilemmas is a game to be played by the whole group. The game involves being presented with situations in which the players have to make difficult decisions. Before you start playing there are a few items to prepare and the rules to go through.

Dilemma cards. Before you can start, each candidate is given five blank cards. On each card, the candidate writes down a question arising from a tricky situation ie a dilemma. If you are not too sure what kinds of tricky situations to invent, then look at the examples given on the facing page.

Prediction cards. Each candidate also needs two prediction cards, one with 'Yes, you would.' and the other with 'No, you wouldn't.' written on it.

How to play. Everyone sits around a table in a circle (or on the floor). Everyone is to have a turn. Decide who is to start. The person whose turn it is, is called the 'poser' as he/she poses one of his/her questions to a named person in the group, called the 'responder'. The responder is allowed to answer, 'Yes, I would.' or 'No, I wouldn't.' 'I don't know' is not allowed.

Before the responder answers, the poser must predict what the response will be. The poser does this by selecting one of the prediction cards and placing it, face down, in the middle of the table. The card is then turned over after the responder has answered and shown to everyone.

If the poser has correctly predicted the response then he/she loses that dilemma card.

If the poser's prediction is incorrect then the poser keeps the card. However, the poser, if he/she wishes, can challenge the truthfulness of the responder's reply by having a short debate. The rest of the group then votes for either the poser or responder. If the poser wins, the card can be discarded. If the poser loses then the card is kept.

When the outcome is decided, the person to the left of the poser now becomes the poser for the next round. The game continues and the winner is the person who gets rid of all their dilemma cards first.

Here are some examples written by other young people to give you an idea of what dilemmas to write. You can use these or come up with your own...

Sample 'Dilemma' cards

- You find in your son's bedroom a hoard of syringes and think he is a drug addict. Do you ask him?

- You have been having an affair with your best friend's husband and become pregnant. Do you tell your husband it is not his child?

- Your neighbour's dog gets run over and you see the driver hide the body in some bushes. Later, the neighbour asks if you've seen her dog. You don't like her. Do you tell her what happened?

- You want to get into a pub. Do you lie about your age?

- A tramp asks you for money to buy food. You have plenty of money on you. Do you give him some money?

- You saw your friend's girlfriend arm in arm with another boy. Do you tell your friend?

- You meet with a friend who is in possession of stolen goods. The police stop you both and he does a runner. Do you tell the police his name?

- You have a friend who wrote graffiti on a school wall. The teacher is blaming you. Do you take the blame?

- Your son has just been expelled from school. Do you go mad? You were once expelled when you were young.

- You find a £10 note in the science lab after a lesson. Do you hand it in to the teacher?

- You find out that your daughter's boyfriend is a drug addict and drug dealer. Do you make her break up the relationship?

- You've seen a friend steal another friend's shirt from his bedroom. Do you tell your friend who has taken the shirt?

- Your daughter wants to go to an all night party where there is a lot of booze and boys. Do you let her go?

Prediction cards

- No, you wouldn't!
- Yes, you would!

Practice Makes Perfect - The game of life.

■ Life is much more than a game. In The Dilemmas game, the decisions you had to make were black and white, right or wrong; in life, this is not so simple, as decisions are often 'grey', less obviously 'right' or 'wrong'.

■ Do not judge others by the decisions they make.

CANDIDATE'S BOOK — 18. DILEMMAS — 39

19 InXs

Body of Evidence
How good is your knowledge of the human body? For instance, do you know the position and relative sizes of the following parts of the body: liver, intestines, heart, lungs, brain? Try sketching these on the outline of the body.

The body is a marvellously engineered machine, so complex that scientists are unable to understand exactly how it works. Our bodies have been given to us 'brand new' by God to serve us during our time on Earth. As we grow older certain parts of the body wear out or cease to function properly due to accidents or disease. Often we can't help this loss of function. There are however a number of ways to avoid harming the body. Quite often we damage the body by doing things to excess. (Now look at 'Ways of damaging the body by excess')

Ways of harming the spirit
Re-examine the ways in which the body could be harmed physically, but this time think about what would be the emotional, psychological and spiritual effects.

Some examples:

i. substance abuse (eg alcohol, drugs, glue-sniffing).

ii. excess of food (eg sweets, fatty foods).

iii. watching too much TV, or excess of computer games.

iv. continual loud noise or music.

v. not exercising your brain by thinking and learning.

vi. excessive use of cosmetics.

Read and discuss Read the following passage from the Bible: 1 Corinthinians 3:16-17 - and discuss what is meant by 'The body is the temple of the Holy Spirit'.

Ways of damaging the body by excess.

Think of the ways that you can damage the body parts by doing things in excess.

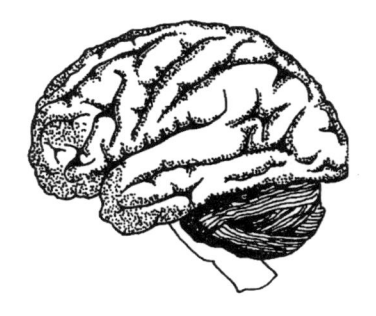

Ways of harming the liver...

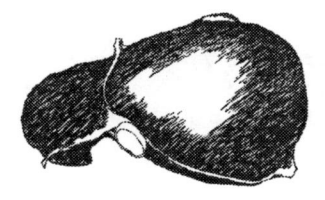

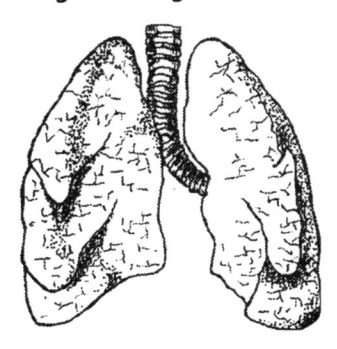

Ways of harming the teeth...

Ways of harming hair and skin...

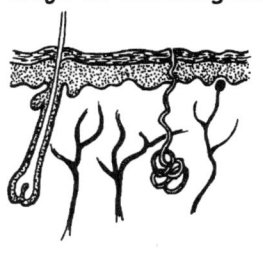

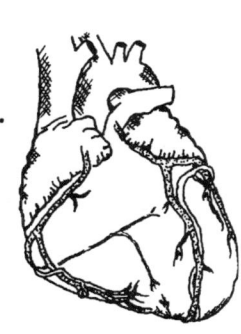

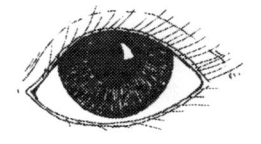

Ways of harming the ears...

Ways of harming the brain...

Ways of harming the heart...

Ways of harming the eyes...

Ways of harming the lungs...

Practice Makes Perfect - Taking care of yourself.

■ Your body is the most important possession that you are truly responsible for. Look after it, exercise it, nourish it properly with good food and by accumulating sound knowledge.

20 SOAPS

Drama 1. Going to a late night party
Cast: Mum, Dad, Dean (a 15 year old), Trish (Dean's 7 year old sister).
Scenario: Dean has been invited to a party by one of his friends. It is expected that the party will go on until 1.00 am. All his other friends will be going and staying late and he wants to go as well.
Characters:
Mum - really anxious person, thinks her son is going to take drugs, get mixed with the wrong crowd etc.
Dad - tries to maintain discipline but feels he is losing his grip on his child.
Dean - cannot see anything wrong, feels like an adult so why not be treated like one; cannot see any dangers; thinks parents are really boring; has to explain to the younger child why she can't go to the party.
Trish - wants to do everything the teenager does; asks to go along to the party; does not really understand what is going on, just wants to join in the discussion.

Drama 3. Smoking
Cast: Helen, Pat, Cath and Linda - all 16 year olds.
Scenario: Four friends idly waiting for a bus. One of them, Cath, lights up a cigarette and this starts a discussion.
Characters:
Helen - attracted to the idea of smoking but knows it's wrong; gives her parents' reasons why smoking is bad.
Pat - strong antismoker and forcefully gives her reasons; her parents are very opposed to smoking as well.
Cath - is a heavy smoker; tried to get the others to smoke; her parents smoke - but they don't know that she does. They would disapprove.
Linda - smokes a certain amount but is suffering from asthma and is trying to give up but finding it really difficult and wishes she had never started.

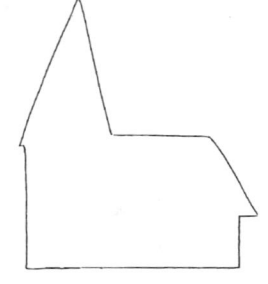

Drama 2. Back of a motorbike
Cast: Jean (a 16 year old), Mum, Grandfather, Billy (Jean's 10 year old brother), Alan (Jean's motorbike-owner friend).
Scenario: Jean has always been interested in motorbikes and has a chance finally to go on the back of a friend's bike - but first she has to get permission from her Mum.
Characters:
Jean - wants to experience the excitement of travelling at speed on a motorcycle. Interrupts her Grandfather when he starts talking about his youth.
Mum - is really anxious; Jean has been foolhardy in the past and has had accidents but Mum does not want to give her reasons why she won't allow it. She also interrupts the Grandfather.
Grandfather - cannot understand the younger generation, but, constantly tries to give an opinion and tells stories of when he was young.
Billy - takes Grandfather's side because he has just given him a bar of chocolate.
Alan - comes in half way through the drama; has been told by Jean that everything has already been sorted out and has come ready to take her for a motorbike ride. He likes Jean's family and does not want to upset them, but he is a really good driver and feels hurt that Mum does not trust him.

Drama 4. Going to Church
Cast: John, Bobby, Jamie (- all 16 year old friends), Fr. Jim.
Scenario: Fr Jim, the parish priest is talking to a group of youngsters about the possibility of starting a Youth Group, but the conversation soon turns around to why young people don't like attending church.
Characters:
John - thinks he should go to church, but does not really enjoy it and feels he doesn't get anything out of it. He likes Fr Jim and does not want to hurt his feelings if he stops going to Church.
Bobby - enjoys going to church but feels embarrassed about it.
Jamie - has given up going to church but still believes in God; he gives his reasons.
Fr. Jim - is a friendly priest who gets on well with young people; he tries to encourage genuine faith and wants a high church attendance.

42 LifeSpan — Coming of Age in the Spirit

Drama 5. All about sex 1

Cast: Trish, Julie, Debbie, Judy - all 15 year olds.
Scenario: This is a conversation between four girls about the pros and cons of having sex with their boyfriends.
Characters:
Trish - is interested in boys, but does not think that sex before marriage is right because she is a Christian. She gives her reasons.
Julie - her older sister is already having sex with her boyfriend. She would like to have a go with her boyfriend! She gives her reasons why she thinks it is OK.
Debbie - is a bit slow on the uptake! She has heard that kissing can make a person pregnant. She does not really understand about sex, but wants to join in the conversation! Her parents are Christians.
Judy - thinks that sex before marriage is a "big" thing to do. She has not yet had sex, but pretends that she has. She is notorious for boasting.

Drama 6. All about sex 2

Cast: Sam, Paul, Hugh (- all 16 year olds).
Scenario: This is a conversation between three boys about sex.
Characters:
Sam - has not got a girlfriend and his friends tease him about being 'unattached'. He wishes he could get a girlfriend and often makes one up to impress his friends.
Paul - has a really good looking girlfriend. Both believe that sex before marriage is wrong because they are Christians. His friends are always making rude suggestions about him and her - which gets him mad!
Hugh - has just split up with his girlfriend because she refused to have sex with him. He was bluffing when he asked her and really regrets what has happened. He is not sure whether sex outside marriage is right or wrong.

Practice Makes Perfect

■ If you identify with any of the situations, listen carefully to the discussion to get ideas which may help you.

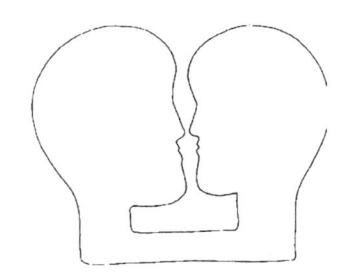

Drama 7. All about sex 3

Cast: James, Charlie, Belinda, Tasha (all 15 year olds).
Scenario: This is a conversation between a group of boys and girls about the freedom of choosing your sexual orientation.
James - is really interested in whether it is alright or not to be gay. He is straight himself.
Charlie - thinks that he might be gay and is really interested in what the Church/God/other people have to say about it. He is very unsure of what his friends would think if he told them.
Belinda - thinks that God considers gay people to be evil because that is what it says in the Bible (Gen 18:16; 19:29 and Rom 1:18-32).
Tasha - thinks that Jesus was a really loving person and would not condemn anyone, regardless of their sexual orientation.

Drama 8. All about sex 4

Cast: Four parents.
Scenario: A conversation between a group of parents.
Characters:
Parent 1 - is a school governor and wants to impress friends with her model lifestyle. However, she is worried that her son is sleeping around. She is anxious to find out about the other parents' children and if they know what their children are up to.
Parent 2 - is a committed Christian and believes that sex outside marriage is not right. He would be horrified to think that his children might be into sex already.
Parent 3 - does not think that there is anything wrong with teenage sex, but is worried that her children might not have sufficient information about how to be careful.
Parent 4 - is very angry because his daughter has just told him she is pregnant. She is 13 years old. He feels she has messed up the rest of her life.

21 'Shopping' Centre

Shopping Centre is an activity which will be explained to you when you arrive. Have fun!

22 Parents' Meeting

Candidate's Questionnaire

Name one thing that you like about your parent(s)...

Name one thing that you dislike about your parent(s)...

Think of 3 good qualities of an ideal parent:
1.
2.
3.

On a scale of 1 to 10 (1 being low - 10 being high) how do you rate your parent(s) on each of the following?...(circle the number you think applies)

a provider	1 2 3 4 5 6 7 8 9 10
a protector	1 2 3 4 5 6 7 8 9 10
a teacher	1 2 3 4 5 6 7 8 9 10
a creator	1 2 3 4 5 6 7 8 9 10
a counsellor	1 2 3 4 5 6 7 8 9 10
a listener	1 2 3 4 5 6 7 8 9 10
a carer	1 2 3 4 5 6 7 8 9 10
a good judge	1 2 3 4 5 6 7 8 9 10

Parents' Questionnaire

Name one thing that you like about your teenage son/daughter...

Name one thing that you dislike about your teenage son/daughter...

Think of 3 good qualities of an ideal teenage son/daughter:
1.
2.
3.

On a scale of 1 to 10 (1 being low - 10 being high) how do you rate <u>your</u> parent(s) on each of the following?...(circle the number you think applies)

a provider	1 2 3 4 5 6 7 8 9 10
a protector	1 2 3 4 5 6 7 8 9 10
a teacher	1 2 3 4 5 6 7 8 9 10
a creator	1 2 3 4 5 6 7 8 9 10
a counsellor	1 2 3 4 5 6 7 8 9 10
a listener	1 2 3 4 5 6 7 8 9 10
a carer	1 2 3 4 5 6 7 8 9 10
a good judge	1 2 3 4 5 6 7 8 9 10

23 LEAVING HOME

Home Alone

- Are you eager to leave home and live in a place of your own or with friends?
- If so, why? Trouble with parents, brothers or sisters?
- Do you just want your independence?
- Do you know of anyone who has just set up home for themselves for the first time?
- What are the main reasons why people leave home?

The Play

The scene:
Two beggars are sitting several feet apart but within talking distance. Each has a hat in front of them, and a sign saying 'homeless'. One is scruffy and ill-kempt, the other is well-dressed and of 'middle-class' appearance. As people walk by they throw small change in the hat.

BEGGAR 1: Been here long?

BEGGAR 2: Nah- I just come at lunchtime- when all the office creeps come out for their sarnies. You?

BEGGAR 1: Been here all day. Not that I've got anything to show for it- 10p and a couple of pesetas, that's all.

BEGGAR 2: That's what you get if you sit outside the travel agents. You should move up a bit. The Oxfam shop is next door. Probably catch a bit of sympathy if you sit there and look pathetic... *(pause)* You left home then?

BEGGAR 1: Yeah- a month ago. Couldn't stand the rows at home, couldn't get on with my folks. You know what parents are like...

BEGGAR 2: No I don't. I was in care. Foster home. I left when I was old enough to get a job. But then I got sick and got the sack 'cos I took too much sick-time off.

BEGGAR 1: But that's disgusting. Couldn't they take you back when you got better?

BEGGAR 2: The thing is, I wont get better. I've got Hepatitis B. I'm a carrier. I'm not sick now, but I can't work in catering. And no one else will take me as I've got no references, a sick record and there's 3 million unemployed!

BEGGAR 1: That makes my story sound a bit silly, really...

BEGGAR 2: Just a minute *(calls out, as if to a passer-by)* 'Scuse me- can you spare some change? *(to BEGGAR 1)* Typical. Don't even give you the time of day. Anyway, you were saying?

BEGGAR 1: I left home because of a row with my Dad. I just got so fed up with him going on at me all the time. I'm the youngest, so he expects me to toe the line. Whatever my brother does, I have to do better. And my brother; how he sucks up to Daddy! *(pulls a face and laughs).*

BEGGAR 2: Well it's your life, mate.

BEGGAR 1: But they're my family. You know, I walked out that day and then changed my mind, but as I was going back I realised I had enough money to keep me going for a while. Dad had opened an account in my name. He gave me the plastic last week for my birthday. *(shows BEGGAR 2 a plastic credit card).*

BEGGAR 2: Well what are you doing here then? *(goes to grab the card).*

BEGGAR 1: It won't get you anywhere - the account's empty. I've spent it all. All two thousand pounds.

BEGGAR 2: Two thousand!? What did you spend it on?

BEGGAR 1: I went on holiday. Club18-30. *(They exchange meaningful looks.)* Then I bought some trainers and jeans and lived in a B-and-B in Torquay after that.

BEGGAR 2: Well, didn't you even try and get a job?

BEGGAR 1: I never thought about it at first. I mean, two thousand pounds is a lot of money- seemed a lot of money. I was just getting round to thinking about a job when the landlady threw me out. I hadn't paid the rent...

BEGGAR 2: *(under his breath)* Deserve everything you get.

BEGGAR 1: Pardon?

BEGGAR 2: I said, you deserve everything you get.

BEGGAR 1: Well at least I'm not a sicko. Hepatitis B. I know where you get that sort of thing from. *(They begin to fight. After a while, they calm down.)*

BEGGAR 1: Look, what are we doing? This is stupid! I'm sorry, I really am. It was a dumb thing to say. I know I've been thick. As a matter of fact, I have been thinking of going home.

BEGGAR 2: Oh surely, and get beaten up by your Old Man!

BEGGAR 1: No, of course not! They're not like that! Sure my Dad can be a pain, but he does care, though he doesn't show it. It'd break his heart to think that I was living like this. *(Indicates the money and sign).* Why don't you come with me.

BEGGAR 2: Nah- it's your family. I couldn't...

BEGGAR 1: 'Course you could. We could put you up for a bit. Just 'til you get sorted out. Come on!

(They pick up their possessions and exit together).

. . . .

Practice Makes Perfect - Make yourself at home.
■ If you have a comfortable home, be thankful.
■ If there are minor troubles at home, realise that it is not easy to run a home, as you'll find out when you have your own place. Therefore don't be obstructive, but help things run smoothly and do your fair share of housework. Try to work through problems - do not just ignore your family sulk.
■ Remember the homeless in your prayers.

Questions

1. Was BEGGAR 1 unwise to leave home because of family problems? What would you have done? What other options are there?

2. Work out in groups of three how much you think it costs to live for a week on your own. Compare notes with the other groups.

3. Would you know what to do if you became sick whilst at work? What would you do if your family were not around?

4. Would you know where to go if you had left home and were having financial problems?

5. Do you think Beggar 1's Dad will allow him to go home? Why/why not?

6. Read together Luke 15:11-31.
Do you think this was a reasonable way for the younger son to behave? Why/why not? Does the father's reaction surprise you? What would you do if you were the father? Is the older son justified in being angry (v. 25 ff.)? Is this a realistic idea of family life? What would you change or preserve in your family in the light of this reading?

24 WHO CARES?

Dear Candidate,

I represent a charity that is planning a new advertising campaign. We are currently short of funds and we may have to reduce the amount of work we do unless we get in more funds.

I am writing to ask you to design a newspaper advert to help launch our campaign. It is hoped that this will increase awareness of our charity and raise more donations. We feel our work is vital and this message needs to be conveyed to the public in a simple yet powerful and original way.

We need an advertising consultant who understands the importance of our work and has the ability to communicate this to others by touching their hearts as well as their minds. I feel that you are that person and we are happy to leave the design of the advert up to you.

Yours sincerely,

Charity Director

List all the Charities you know...

Which one charity would you like to design the advert for and why?

An Example Charity Advert...

No Home
No Fun!
House against homelessness
The facts
What we do...
How you can help us...

Photograph/drawing.
A powerful picture that will have an impact on the readers.

The facts
A list of facts & figures showing the scale of the problems.

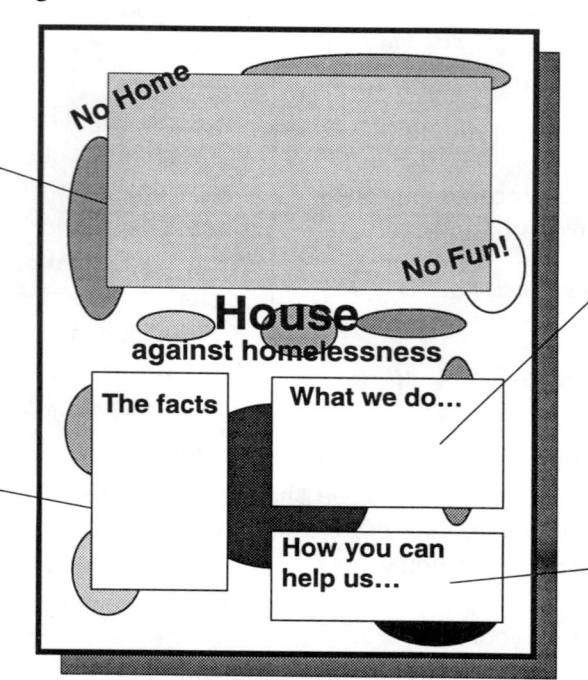

Us..
A summary of the charity & the work it does.

Help !.
What the readers can do to help, eg give money, volunteer, etc.

CAMPAIGN COUNTDOWN

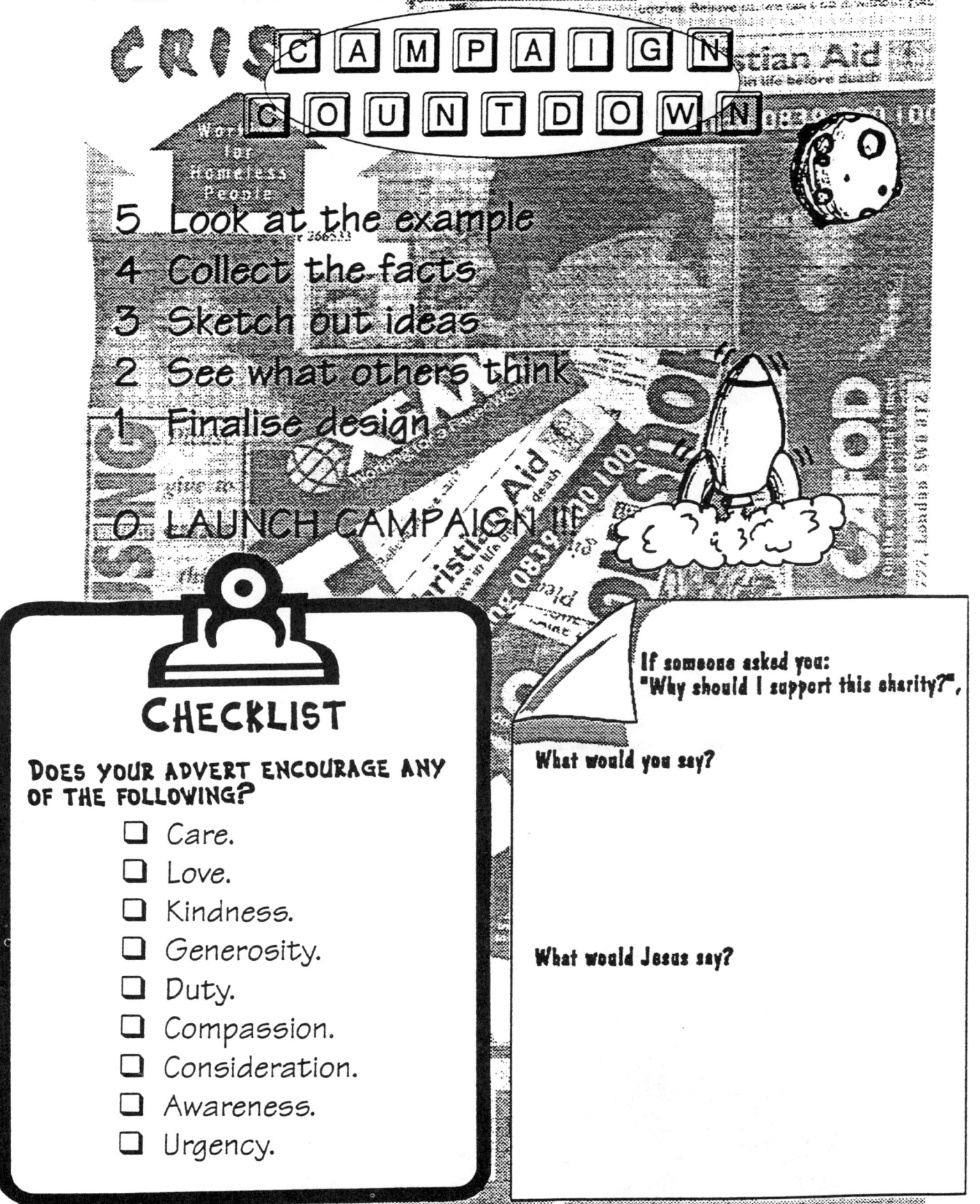

5 Look at the example
4 Collect the facts
3 Sketch out ideas
2 See what others think
1 Finalise design
0 LAUNCH CAMPAIGN !!!

CHECKLIST

DOES YOUR ADVERT ENCOURAGE ANY OF THE FOLLOWING?

- ☐ Care.
- ☐ Love.
- ☐ Kindness.
- ☐ Generosity.
- ☐ Duty.
- ☐ Compassion.
- ☐ Consideration.
- ☐ Awareness.
- ☐ Urgency.

If someone asked you: "Why should I support this charity?",

What would you say?

What would Jesus say?

CANDIDATE'S BOOK　　　WHO CARES?　49

25 ChildIIAdult

Same difference!

Most people know the difference between men and women and between boys and girls. But what distinguishes a child from an adult? Make a list of distinct differences between:

1. a baby and a small child.

2. a small child and a 12 year old.

3. a 12 year old and a 16 year old.

4. a 16 year old and an adult.

Do you consider yourself an adult?

- if yes, then do you look like an adult?

- if no, what do you 'need' to be an adult?

Look at other societies and cultures and how they view differences between children and adults...

Indian Rajput

The Hindu culture in India has a custom for princes to celebrate the change from childhood to 'Brachmachari' (the first stage of manhood). The young prince rides through the streets wearing his father's clothes, which signifies his new status and shows publicly that he can now study the Hindu scriptures. He is also given "the sacred thread" which the higher castes wear to show their "spiritual birth".

Bar Mitzvah

Bar Mitzvah means 'son of the commandments' in Hebrew. For centuries Jewish boys celebrated Bar Mitzvah when they reached 13 years of age. To prepare for the ceremony the boys have to study the Torah, the prophets and the writings (what Christians know as the Old Testament). During the ceremony, in front of the whole community, they must read aloud certain parts of this Scripture - it is often the most important day of their life! From then on it is each boy's responsibility to keep the laws written in Scripture. Nowadays, in some Jewish communities, girls have an equivalent ceremony called a Bat Mitzvah.

The Gisu of East Africa

Circumcision is a common practice in African tribes to mark the change from childhood to adulthood. For instance, in the Gisu tribe of East Uganda a boy is circumcised when he is seventeen years old, watched by a crowd of male friends and relatives. It is really important that the boy undergoes the ordeal without flinching. Even today, educated Gisu believe they must undergo circumcision to be seen as mature men.

Ox-name

There is a tribe in Africa called the Dinka tribe. When the young men of the village are about to reach adulthood they undergo an initiation rite in which they are given the name of an ox! The tribe, from its early history, was a herding people and their very existence relied on keeping cattle. When boys reach adulthood they must join the other men and take on the responsibility of keeping the tribe alive. With their 'ox-name' the young men recognise their links with the past and promise to carry on their tradition. They are now full members of the tribe and must protect the others.

The Mehinachu tribe of Brazil

In some societies young people must undergo a period of seclusion in which they are taught the 'mysteries of life' before they can be accepted as adults. The physical changes are not the only important factors but also what they know about life. For example, in Brazil, the Mehinachu girls are put in a darkened hut for six months. They emerge with pale skins and long, unkempt hair. They can now be treated as women and can get married.

Think up a modern day 'ritual' for our society to mark the coming of age.

The Bemba of Northern Zambia

Some people believe it is necessary to prove adulthood by showing a skill or talent, especially one useful to society. Boys in the Memba tribe are required to show that they can hunt animals successfully. None of the boy's family are allowed to eat the meat of his first kill. But with the second kill, the boy and his father can eat of the meat. The third kill is just for the boy himself, who is now considered a man.

The Masai of Africa

Many African tribes organise their people into 'age sets'. As a child a Masai boy does not have much responsibility, but this changes as he gets older. At the age of fourteen a boy is circumcised to show that he is now a man.

The Metuktire of Amazonia

There are often symbols in societies which represent maturity. In Amazonian tribes the traditional symbol for men is a pierced or ornamented lower lip. The Metuktire tribe have as their symbol a flat circular disc known as a lip-plug, which is meant to show their ability as warriors and orators. This tradition is now dying out and the lip plug is being replaced by a short string of beads threaded through the lower lip.

Practice Makes Perfect - Back to the present.

■ Many people spend much time 'looking forward'. It is good to hope in the future but do not ignore the present. Try to make the most of today.

26 RELATIONSHIPS

1 DON'T CHEAT THE PERSON IN THE MIRROR

1. The mirror never lies
Look at yourself in a mirror and write down 3 positive and 3 negative points about yourself that other people don't know:

Positive:
-
-
-

Negative:
-
-
-

2. Mirror image
Think of your reflection as a person who knows you intimately. What sort of reference would he/she give you for a job?

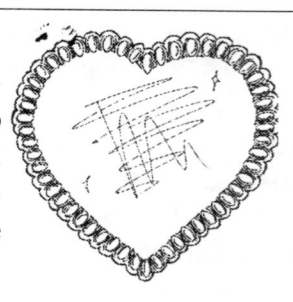

3. Hall of Mirrors
Have you ever been to the Hall of Mirrors at a funfair - where your image is distorted by the different mirrors? Like these mirrors, people don't see us as we really are. What can we do about this?

4. In the image of God
We are created in our own unique way by God. He loves us and blessed us with talents and gifts. He sent His son Jesus to us that we may have life and have it to the full.

What sort of image has Jesus got of you?

5. Into the future
When you look in the mirror you see yourself as you are now. How do you imagine how you will change in 10 years time, 20 years, when you are 75 years old?

6. Catchphrase
Make up a motto or catchphrase that sums you up.

52 LifeSpan · Coming of Age in the Spirit

② DESERT ISLAND FRIENDS

The Challenge

In many cultures, young people are set challenges to prove they are worthy of becoming adults. Imagine that you belong to a community which has set you a challenge to test if you should gain adult status. The challenge is to spend four weeks on a desert island. You are allowed to take four other people with you and you can also take all necessary provisions. When you select who and what to take, keep in mind any adverse conditions, poor facilities and possible difficulties which may arise. You therefore need to choose the four people carefully.

In the table below list four people who you would take, the particular talent or skill they could offer and the task you would set them.

Name	Particular talent or skill	Task given
1.		
2.		
3.		
4.		

Week One

The first four days are a great novelty and all is going relatively well with everybody contributing. On day six there is tension. There is an obvious personality clash between two people who are both important to the overall good of the group. As leader, you need to tackle the problem quickly.
1. Who might these two people be?
2. What would be the problem?
3. How could you tackle the problem?

Week Three

At the end of the third week you are 'rescued' from the island. When you return to your home the 'elders' or wise people of the community hand you a list and ask you to grade yourself on how well you performed as a leader. For each of the following, grade yourself on a scale 1 to 10, where 1 is very poor and 10 is extremely good.

Think of other qualities that are important in leading others.
How can some of these qualities be put into practice by you in your home?

Week Two

Week two was really hard - bad weather, tiredness, hard to wash and dry clothes, some food running out, and people reluctant to cooperate. You decide to spend one day on your own. At one point you become acutely aware of home and think of the people you've left behind.
1. Who might these people be? (use fictitious names if you do not want to use their actual names).
2. What could they offer you now?

Ability to:	Grade 1-10
1. Listen to others. 2. Cooperate with others. 3. Motivate staff. 4. Motivate others. 5. Forgive. 6. Bring healing to difficult situations. 7. Be punctual.	

CANDIDATE'S BOOK 26. RELATIONSHIPS. 53

3 CASH TO CARRY

(1) Entrepreneur's paradise - youth

At the end of a week's 'think tank' on youth, a group of business people came up with what they considered important facts about young people. Listed below are 6 facts they thought would be of most benefit to them if they were to launch a new youth product:

1. Young people have money or can get it from their parents.
2. They are not always mature or thrifty with money.
3. They are impressionable.
4. They like to have or gather things especially if these things project the right image, give an air of self worth or importance and give a sense of belonging.
5. As business people, we can create a product which is new, better and attractive.
6. Through good marketing and advertising we can create a need for a product, do a quick sell and invest the profits in yet another equally irresistible product.

We are on to a winner!

(2) Spending spree

Imagine that you have won a competition in which the prize is a complete outfit of any clothes of your choice. Draw up a list of the clothes you would want, then work out the total cost.

(3) Brand names

Write down as many brand names as you can in 1 minute. Compare your list with the other candidates.

(4) Have you ever been 'seduced' in the following way?

Imagine you are standing and looking at a shop window displaying a really attractive hi-fi system. What are the thoughts that go through your head?

a. "I don't need that. I have a good cassette/radio player at home."

b. "It looks very good, very compact, remote control, stereo. It would fit beautifully on the little shelf in my room."

c. "It would be very useful for direct taping, good sound quality too. I could do with it and I'm sure it would give me much enjoyment."

d. "Yes, I could do with that, in fact it's what I've been looking for. I'll buy it!"

e. "I must get it. I'll ask Mum to get it for my birthday."

(5) More-more-more and killed for choice

Where is your favourite shopping place? Go for an imaginary walk about there. List all the shops which sell products specially aimed at young people. Having done this, (name them) put an 'x' on those which are in no way necessary and you could live without.

In your home:
• think of the things that you or your family have bought in the last three years that have either not been used or have not been necessary.
• is one reason because they have become that outdated already?

Discuss your ideas with the group.

Levis Alone

Can you remember the adverts used to sell Levi jeans? Here's a reminder:

1985 A young guy undresses in a laundrette to 'Heard it on the Grapevine'.
1985 A guy jumps in a bath to shrink his jeans, 'What a Wonderful World' plays in the background.
1987-9 Eddie Kidd slips by bouncer at nightclub, 'Stand by Me' reaches No. 1. Later that year, a tearful girl puts on jeans left by her boyfriend, 'When a Man Loves a Woman' enters the charts.
1990 Beautiful girl on beach caught by dog trying to steal a surfer's jeans. Happy ending as all three waggle off into the sunset to 'Can't Get Enough of Your Love' by Bad Company. Biker drives into stockbroker's office and gives jeans to redhead who yanks off her skirt, pulls on the jeans and rides off with him. Steve Miller's 'The Joker' reaches No. 1.
1991 Pool-hall hero beats fat man and gets him to drop his trousers to the Clash's 'Should I Stay or Should I Go?'. Another No. 1. 'Thelma and Louise' actor Brad Pitt gets out of jail into arms of lover waiting with camera and Levis. T-Rex '20th Century Boy' goes to No. 10.
1992 Bronzed son of former Miss America makes a splash as he dives in backyard swimming pools in jeans to Dinah Washington's 'Mad About the Boy'. Then modern-day Cinderella tries to find the mysterious owner of a pair of Levis. She sees a half-naked boy in a garage. Irma Franklin's 'Piece of My Heart' goes to No. 1.

(extracts taken from 'The Daily Mirror' Thursday 4th February 1993).

(6) Advertising

■ What are your favourite adverts and what makes them memorable to you?
■ What makes a good advert?

Advertisements are largely fantasy, imaginary, unreal; even though they try to sell real products. Have you ever seen:
- a drunk man in an alcohol advert?
- an old-looking woman used to advertise moisturising cream which claims to keep you looking young?
- the latest car on the market breaking down?
- an excessively fat person advertising chocolate?

Can you think of other more 'truthful adverts' that could be produced?

(7) An ever changing world

Everything around us seems to keep changing. The latest gear soon becomes outdated and our happiness becomes disappointment when something new comes out to rival it.

Can you think of anything that does not change or changes very little with time?

(8) Private resolutions for simplicity

Does materialism and consumerism really bring true happiness? Many people find materialism really unsatisfying and yearn for a 'simpler' life. What does this form of 'simplicity' mean? If you were to lead a 'simpler' life what changes would you have to make to your lifestyle? Think about this in terms of your:
- use of time,
- eating habits,
- prayer life,
- community involvement,
- room,
- clothes,
- leisure,
- entertainment.

(9) The life and message of Christ

What can we learn from the Scriptures? Look up the following passages in the Bible and think about the message Jesus is putting across to us: Matt 20:16-30, 4:1-11, 6:19-33, 18:1-4.

Jesus could have had anything He wanted - why then did He lead a simple life? Think about:
- what Jesus would say about today's world and its values?
- what should the Church say or do about society's values?
- how should the Church be seen in today's world?
- how does Jesus ask us to live our lives and why?

4 ROOM INSIDE - ROOM OUTSIDE

1. Your own room
You may or may not have a bedroom of your own. Either way, if you could plan your room what would it be like?
■ Draw a plan of your ideal bedroom.
■ How would you like friends and visitors to treat your room?
■ How would you feel if your room was broken into and ransacked?

2. Survey
Take an imaginary look around your ideal room and list the various items which had their source elsewhere in the table below. One example is included:

Item	Main orginal source	Geographical origin	Describe the process of change from the orginal form to present form
chair	tree	Rain forest	from cutting down tree to carpentry

3. One Big Room ... The Wild Animal
The Earth is like one big room where billions of living things co-exist alongside each other in wonderful rhythm and harmony. However, some of the inhabitants are endangered by humanity's exploitation of the planet. Choose a threatened species and imagine a conversation with one of its individuals. What would it say on the following:
• How does it see its 'room'?
• What does it see happening to its 'room' due to pollution etc?
• It makes a plea on behalf of all wildlife with whom it shares its room outside. Imagine what the animal would say.

4. How much do you know?

Do you know the causes and effects of: acid rain, desertification, poison in food chains, greenhouse effect, carbon monoxide, smog and effluent?

Did you know that:

- there are 50 nuclear stations in Moscow alone;

- an explosion at a chemical factory in Bhopal, India killed about 2,500 people and disabled a further 2000;

- accidents have occurred at nuclear stations at Pennsylvania, Chernobyl and Selafield;

- plutonium has been dumped in the Irish sea;

- oxygen is on sale in Tokyo to combat pollution's effect on people's breathing;

- gas and oil supplies could be depleted by the year 2050;

- chemicals and insecticides used in the control of weeds and insects can damage and infect food;

- overfishing and extensive hunting have resulted in the depletion of fish in or seas and many species of wildlife;

5. The Christian Viewpoint

Take time to reflect on the following passages: Psalm 8, Rom 8:22-23, John 13:12-15.

5 People's Church

1. Letter to a Buddhist
A young Buddhist knows you were Confirmed recently. He wants to know more about the Church and asks the following questions:
- What is it?
- What and when did it start?
- Does it serve a purpose?
- Could it have a place in my life?
- Would I have a role in its life?

2. Trace the progression
Trace the progression from the Annunciation of the birth of Jesus to the story of the Early Church using a copy of the New Testament by searching for the references given. Write one or two words to sum up the reference.

God the Father   John 1:1-3   John 3:16

Jesus   Luke 1:26-38   Luke 2:1-7
           Luke 4:1-15   John 17:3 and 4.

Apostles   Luke 6:12-16   Luke 9:1-6
           Luke 24:46-53 Matt 28:16-20

Church (Christ continues His presence through the Holy Spirit)
Beginnings:
           Acts 1:12-14   Acts 2:1
           Acts 6:1-7   Acts 13:1-5
           Acts 15:1-12

Church today: Sacraments
                Hierarchy
                People

All these help the continuation and growth of the Church today.

3. Saints and sinners
In small groups, discuss the following points:
- the Church is made up of saints and sinners.
- the Church is obliged to preserve and pass on the values and teachings of Christ.
- the Church is irrelevant in today's world.
- everybody belongs in the Church.
- the Church should get involved in political issues.
- the Church is a weakening institution among stronger more powerful institutions.
- the Church is a sign of hope and peace.

4. Us - the Church

How do you get on with your local church? Write down some positive and negative words associated with the church in your experience:

In your group, draw up some guide lines which you think would improve your local church. For example, what are people's needs? How could you meet those needs?

5. What a priest thinks

Here are some comments made by a priest about young people and their relationships with the church in today's world. Do you agree or disagree?
- young people find the Church formal and 'adult'.
- apart from major celebrations like Baptisms, first communions, Confirmations, weddings and funerals their lives are untouched by the Church.
- the peer pressure not to participate in the life of the church is immense.
- many young people have no foundational faith, so the Church is irrelevant.
- there are many more interesting, sociable and fun things to do.
- many don't practice their beliefs because their mother/father, brother/sister does not or do not practice so there is no family support for the faith.
- occasionally, there seems to be an increase or revival in the number of Christians.
- some young people become very committed and involved in the Church.
- after a period of rejection, doubt, disillusionment, and searching some young people find meaning and a home in the Church.
- young people need help and encouragement to appreciate the church.

Positive	Negative

6. Preparation for Celebration of Affirmation

- You are important in the Church and so is everyone else. 'Love your neighbour as yourself.' Look through your workbook and decide on what you could offer to the Church. Make it specific and choose one area you would like to try out in the coming year. It might be physical, for example helping others, or spiritual, for example encouraging others.

  When you have chosen an area, write it down and be prepared to include it in the service of Affirmation.

- Your favourite passage of Scripture. If you have a favourite, practice reading it to include in the service. Or if your group is large, write it down and display it on a noticeboard.

27. CELEBRATION OF AFFIRMATION

> The Celebration of Affirmation takes place within Catholic Mass or Anglican Holy Communion. Those parts of the service are outlined below.

You will be instructed what to do during rehearsals for this ceremony

THE WELCOME / GREETING

Candidate: On behalf of the group of young people celebrating their Affirmation today, I would like to welcome our parents, family, and friends from the rest of the community. Today marks an important stage in our lives when we will take on a greater responsibility for our Faith. With the help of the Gifts of the Holy Spirit we will be accepting our adult status in the Church and making a commitment to try to follow Christ.

V *Priest:* The Lord be with you.
R *All:* **And also with you.**

V *Candidate:* Thus says the Lord; I shall be your God.
R *All:* **We shall be your people.**

V *Candidate:* God has told you what is good; and what He requires of you. To do justice to love kindness and to walk humbly with the Lord your God.
R *All:* **We shall be your people.**

V *Candidate:* Thus says the Lord; the righteous walk in integrity. Happy are the children who follow them.
R *All:* **We shall be your people.**

V *Candidate:* Thus says the Lord; listen my people to my teaching.
R *All:* **We shall be your people.**

PENITENTIAL RITE - OR PRAYERS OF PENITENCE

MINISTRY/LITURGY OF THE WORD

First reading: Jer 1:4-10.

Second reading: 1 Cor 12:12-27.

Gospel: Matt 28:16-20.

HOMILY BY CATECHIST

THE AFFIRMATION

Priest: At Baptism (in ancient times) touching ears and mouth, the priest prayed that, as newly baptised, you would soon listen to the Word of God and proclaim it in your lives. Now, by the same symbolic action you are being commissioned to go forth, to listen and proclaim that same Word of God as adults.

The catechist calls up each of candidate by name.

As the candidates come forward, the priest touches their ears and mouth saying.

Priest: Ephthatha - be opened.

(If there are any who are deaf and/or dumb or do not wish their ears and mouth touched then the priest can touch their hands and head.)

When this part is completed each candidate shares their personal Scriptural text and Ministry with the community. This is done by either:

a. reading out one or two sentences of their chosen piece of Scripture and announcing their chosen Ministry,

b. or the Scriptural text and their Ministry can be written down and stuck to a large piece of paper somewhere in the church.

The priest explains what has occurred.

Priest: The candidates have chosen a passage of Scripture that has spoken to them in some meaningful way and they have committed themselves to one area of Ministry which they wish to fulfil. These have been written down and are now pinned to the board. I invite all of you to read these intentions after the service and to pray that they may have the strength to carry out their Ministry.

While this part of the ceremony is occurring a hymn can be sung - ('I the Lord of Sea and Sky' is appropriate.)

THE 'DECOMMISSIONING' OF THE CATECHIST(S)

The priest calls the catechist(s) out by name. The catechist(s) come to the front of the church.

Priest: The catechist(s) has (have) represented the community in assisting the young people prepare, not only for today, but also for their future spiritual life. We would like to thank the catechist(s) for all his (her/their) hard work and efforts. We thank God for their example and Ministry to our young people.

The catechist(s) who was (were) sitting at the front, return(s) to the body of the church to rejoin the congregation.

The Prayer of the Faithful

The Peace

The Offertory

Priest: Our offering, to the Lord and to each other before we approach the altar is peace. The peace of the Lord be always with you.

All: **And also with you.**

The Liturgy of the Eucharist

Proper preface:
Priest: "Father, all powerful and everliving God, we do well always and everywhere to give you thanks through Jesus Christ Our Lord. We thank you especially today for the life, growth and love of our young people. We delighted at their birth. We were proud and joyful at their Baptism. We have celebrated the various stages of their development. We have been happy to watch them grow, play, achieve, make friends.

Today we are delighted, happy, proud, joyful, because we gather to celebrate their having reached adulthood. We celebrate all these years of togetherness, support and love which have moved our young people towards this great moment; their coming of age in the Spirit.

This is a moment of communion, when we unite in our Christian adulthood; a new beginning, a chance for the Church, a moment when You bless us all, Father. In thanksgiving and celebration we say… "Holy, holy, holy…"

The Lord's Prayer

Communion Prayer

Post Communion sentence:
For you shall go to all to whom I send you, and you shall speak whatever I command you, for I am with you to deliver you, says the Lord.

The Communion

The Concluding Rite